The Cat on My Shoulder

THE
Cat ON MY Shoulder

Lisa Angowski Rogak

THE CAT ON MY SHOULDER

Published by Longmeadow Press, 201 High Ridge Road, Stamford,
CT 06904.

Interior design by Richard Oriolo

Library of Congress Cataloging-in-Publication Data

Rogak, Lisa Angowski.
    Cat on my shoulder / by Lisa Rogak. — 1st ed.
        p.   cm.
    ISBN: 0-681-41458-8
    1. Authors, American—20th century—Biography. 2. Pet
owners—United States—Biography. 3. Cats—United States—
Anecdotes.
    I. Title.
    PS129.R65   1992
810.9'0054—dc20
[B]   92-31333
                                                               CIP

Printed in the United States

First Edition

0 9 8 7 6 5 4 3 2 1

To my father
Louis Anthony Angowski
(1924–1974)

Contents

The Cat on My Shoulder

Introduction

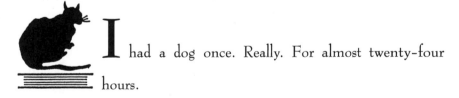 I had a dog once. Really. For almost twenty-four hours.

Then I gave it back.

You just *know* you're a cat person, even years before you have your first cat, just as some people know they were born to be writers.

More often than not, these two qualities occupy space in one soul. Writers and cats seem to be custom-made for each other. A writer is quiet when working. A cat—whose primary occupation is sleeping—is silent, too. Writers tend to be loners. The same with cats.

A writer pounces on words; a cat pounces on members of the rodent kingdom.

Writers can become jealous when the spotlight is on somebody else, but only when they want the spotlight to be on themselves at that particular moment. The rest of the time, they couldn't care less. Ditto the cat.

And when a writer receives praise, he or she stretches out, stands a little straighter, and sometimes purrs. A cat, when petted, reacts the same way.

Just about the only way cats and writers aren't compatible is when there's a computer between them. The cat jumps up, walks across the keyboard, bites the floppy disk, sits atop the warm monitor, and, of course, sheds.

That's why some of us still write with pencils.

The Cat on My Shoulder tells of the relationship between writers and their cats. During research for the book, only a few writers I approached turned out not to be cat people. (I'll protect their identites from readers who might be disappointed or irate.) Indeed, most authors I contacted turned out to be very happy for a chance to talk about their favorite companions' influence on their work.

Naturally, the responses I received were as varied as the authors themselves. Several writers were content with one cat; for others, seven is not enough. Some used cats for inspiration and required their presence at the word processor; others banished cats from their workroom, interacting with their pets purely on a social level.

One question I frequently asked writers was, Do you think cats are psychic? Some laughed at this; others very definitely nodded their heads over the phone. I'm psychic, so I knew that their heads were bobbing. While I was writing the book and conducting the interviews, the neighborhood cats would roam around the converted barn where I work and squint through the glass doors to see what was going on. They *knew* I was writing about cats; they never come around when I'm writing about arthritis or Vermont, for example. I think they just wanted to make sure I was representing their peers fairly.

Two of my cats are house cats, however, and they resented this intrusion into their space. Either that, or they were incredibly jealous of the outside cats. Anyway, when I was on the phone interviewing science fiction writer Joe Haldeman, all of a sudden I heard this ungodly noise not four feet from my desk. My fat, pushy cat Squggy was conducting a mean howling and spitting session with one of the neighbor's barn cats—a cat that's even bigger than Squggy. When I played back the tape, I couldn't hear what Joe was saying. After I hung up, I wiped a lot of cat spit off the doors to let the sun through again. Squggy means business.

The only way to really complete this book is to get another cat. And since most of the writers I interviewed either already had a Maine coon cat, envied someone else's, or planned to get one of their own, a Maine coon cat it is. I think I'll name it Epson, after my computer.

LISA ANGOWSKI ROGAK
Enfield, New Hampshire

A Brief
History of Writers
and Cats

Writers and cats have long been associated with each other, serving as companion and inspiration. Writers both famous and obscure have worked with cats on their shoulders and laps. Millions of cats have undoubtedly walked across millions of computer and typewriter keyboards, and have teethed on tens of thousands of pens. (Rumor has it they prefer Mont Blancs.) Cats generally do their best to distract a writer from her true calling to allow the designated human can opener to focus on what's really important: their feline selves.

Most of the time, it works.

Henry James worked with a cat on his shoulder. So did Charles Dickens. In fact, when Dickens' cat thought his master had written enough for the day, he would reach over with his paw and snuff out the candle flame.

At one point, Ernest Hemingway had thirty cats underfoot in his house in Cuba; he appeared to be fonder of his cats than his wife, Mary. She took it upon herself to create some semblance of normality in the household and directed the construction of a three-story stone tower across the courtyard from the main house. Each floor of the tower was designed for a specific purpose: one would provide a writing space for her husband; another would give her a secluded aerie where she could lie out in the sun in the nude; another would belong solely to the cats. Most of the cats accepted her generous offer and moved into the cat house, although some preferred to stay in the main house.

Edgar Allan Poe wrote the classic horror story, *The Black Cat*, which has been analyzed and anthologized countless times. When his wife Virginia was dying of consumption, they were so poor they couldn't afford a blanket. He used his winter coat to cover her, and their cat, Catterina, provided additional warmth by sitting on Virginia's chest.

The French writer Colette was one of the world's greatest lovers of cats. She wrote a novel about a cat, *La Chatte, (The Cat)*, and included cats in many of her stories. Once, in New York City, she saw a cat sitting in the street. She walked over to it and proceeded to meow at it. The cat responded in kind. Colette then exclaimed to a companion, "Finally! Someone who speaks French!"

T. S. Eliot, of course, is probably the most famous writer with cats. Besides penning *Old Possum's Book of Practical Cats*, which provided the basis for the Broadway musical *Cats*, Eliot wrote other poems about felines. In "The Naming of Cats," he decreed that a cat should have three names: one suitable for everyday use; another "particular, peculiar, and more dignified," and a third "you never will guess and the cat will never confess."

Other literary cat lovers over the years have included Victor Hugo,

Abraham Lincoln, William Cowper, William Shakespeare, and Honoré de Balzac.

Famous literary references to cats include "For I will consider my cat Jeoffry," by Christopher Smart in his poem "Jubilate Agno," which he wrote in prison, with his cat Jeoffry as his sole companion; "On the Death of a Favorite Cat Drowned in a Tub of Gold-Fishes," by Thomas Gray; "Last Words to a Dumb Friend," which served as an epitaph, by Thomas Hardy; *Tobermory* by Saki, the pen name for H. H. Munro; Rudyard Kipling's story *The Cat Who Walked by Himself*; and Lewis Carroll's Cheshire Cat in *Alice's Adventures in Wonderland*.

Perhaps the fundamental connection that can be made between writers and cats is perfectly summed up in a statement by Nelson Antrim Crawford in his essay "Cats Holy and Profane" in his book *Cats in Prose and Verse*, published by Coward-McCann in 1947. He wrote, "In nearly all lovers of cats one finds a certain contempt for the stupidity of mankind."

Alice Adams

I grew up in North Carolina in a house out in the country and we had cats. They usually stayed down in the basement where the furnace was.

I think I like cats because I grew up in the country where a good supply of dogs and cats were taken for granted. I've been living in the city, and have had them here since my son was little. I had a strong idea that kids should have pets. Cats are a lot easier to cope with in cities than dogs. At this point, I live in a fairly big house with a yard, so my cats *could* go out, but I don't let them. It's too risky.

At the moment, I only have two cats, Sam, a nine-month-old Maine coon cat, and Black, who's seventeen years old and half Burmese. My problem is that Black hates Sam. She longs for his death.

My favorite was a cat named Ferg; I had her for seventeen years. Twenty years ago, I went to a lunch party and fell madly in love with this absolutely beautiful Abyssinian cat, and the hostess said, "Guess what? She got out on the street and met someone." So we chose one of her kittens and named it Ferg. She was half Manx and half Abyssinian. She was so cross and haughty and independent—I loved her.

I have friends who would say that my cats run my house, but it doesn't seem that way to me. But Ferg was very adamant about when it was time for me to work, and she was usually right. She would go into my study before I arrived. Ferg would sit on top of the manuscripts on my desk, or in my lap when I was typing. She thought everything I wrote was for her. Sam and Black don't spend much time in my study.

I don't think cat lovers are that shameless. I think that some of us have been somewhat embarrassed by non-cat lovers, although I have to say that I find a love of cats a very sympathetic quality in people. And conversely, I wonder about people who really dislike cats. I had an interesting conversation with a good friend who's an editor in New York and adores cats. We talked about men, in particular, who disliked cats. We decided that men who don't like cats are apt to be bullies, because one of the points about cats is that you can't possibly bully them. And we cited a man who is an editor, whom we both have reason to dislike quite a lot, who hates cats. We decided that is because he is a bully.

Last year I decided that I wanted a Maine coon cat for my birthday, so I called several people. I called one woman at a cattery who sounded quite pleasant, but she said she was quite fussy about who they sell them to. I found that perfectly understandable, but I said my credentials as a cat lover are really quite excellent. I told her, for instance, that I'm sixty-five years old, and that all my life I've had cats. There was a very long pause, and then she said, "Oh, you're sixty-five? Who will take care of the cat when you pass on? That seemed to me to be carrying cat love a little too far. So I told her I have a son who was forty who will be inheriting it.

Unfortunately, I have a suspicion that Maine coon cats are a kind of new fad. One reason I like them is that when I was a child I spent lots of time in Maine, and so I am crazy about anything connected with Maine. The very idea of a Maine coon cat was infinitely attractive.

Then I went to a cat show and saw Maine coon cats for the first time. They're extremely nice. One editor friend of mine, a man who loves cats and dogs but really prefers dogs, thinks that Maine coon cats are actually dogs. He refers to Sam as my dog in cat clothes. Because he likes him so much, this is his version of a compliment.

Alice Adams

Alice Adams is a novelist living in San Francisco. Her novels include *Superior Women* and *Second Chances*.

Lloyd Alexander

We only have two cats now. One is a black-and-white named William Smallcat; the other is a little tortoiseshell named Nik the Fat Kitten. Before William arrived, I had a black-and-white cat named Roger the Badger. We were inseparable for twelve years; then he died, and I thought that's it, no new cats, no new heartbreak. A year later, almost to the day he died, a black-and-white cat showed up in the backyard, and I chased him away. He didn't leave, and to my eternal shame, I threw clods of mud at him. He kept popping out of the bushes with this big happy expression on his face, like, "Hey, don't you know me?" After a couple of weeks there was a terrible thunderstorm, and I had to let him into the house. We have been devoted to each other ever since.

I close my workroom door, but they put their paws under it and I have to let them in. They walk on the table and over the typewriter and under the sofa. They poke into everything and eventually get bored and leave. They just like to check things out.

The interesting thing about Nik the Fat Kitten is that a few months before she showed up, our old tortoiseshell, Tiger, who was almost twenty years old, died. A few months later, here comes a stray tortoiseshell. So I've replaced my black-and-white and a tortoiseshell with another black-and-white and a tortoiseshell.

One of my earliest books for adults, *My Five Tigers,* was about our cats, and it's considered a cat classic. When I began writing for young people, my first fantasy, published in 1964, was called *Time Cat.* It's about a boy and his cat who traveled back in time to nine historical periods. They traveled to places a cat would like to visit, where cats were pampered and worshipped, such as eighth-century Japan and ancient Egypt.

I'll always try to sneak a cat into what I'm writing. It's my private trademark. If I can include a cat, I'll do it.

Actually, I was an ailurophobe for years. I was a dog person because I was never brought up with cats. In the mid-forties, years later, when we married, my wife said, "We're going to have cats," which I thought was terrible. She insisted and brought in a brown tabby. The instant I saw him I was converted. One was not enough. After my first novel my publisher asked me, "What's next?" In sudden inspiration, I told him I was going to write a book about cats. He said, "That's great," and *My Five Tigers* was my second book.

I think cats are more easily mythologized than dogs. It's easier for humans to make up a whole mythology and play games with what we've invented about cats. I have long philosophical conversations with William about the nature of woodles. Don't ask me about what a woodle is; it's one of these silly things that pop into my mind. And we speculate, do they really exist? *Cogito ergo woodle.* Sometimes I have mental conversations with him, but sometimes I talk aloud, and am absolutely silly. I think this is part of the mythologizing process, pretending that he understands what I'm saying.

I think what we're all trying to do is rationalize what is essentially not rationalizable; that is, why we love these animals more than any other. And we come up with a rationale: they're beautiful, they're intelligent, they're independent. We can go on and on, and it really doesn't get to the heart of it. I couldn't say why I love cats any more than why I love Mozart instead of Mahler. I can't explain why we fall in love with someone. That's just the way it is.

Being a shameless cat lover has to do with being defensive about our very lives. The most vocal cat lovers have been writers, for the simple reason that they have means of expressing it. There are millions of unheard cat lovers who don't have any access to writing about them. Also, writers are outcasts and thus are on the defensive. Like cats, they're essentially rebels. One thing a cat is not is obedient. Writers aren't either, at least not the good ones.

The only thing I don't like about cats is that I can't always find them when I'm looking for them. If I call them, they probably won't come. I'm not trying to exercise power over them, I just want to know where the hell they are.

I prefer cats to human company most of the time. I have never seen a cat do a stupid thing; I can't say the same about human beings.

Lloyd Alexander has written over thirty books of fiction and nonfiction for adults and young people, and has translated works by Sartre. His many awards include the Newbery Medal, the National Book Award, the American Book Award, and the National Jewish Book Award. He lives in Drexel Hill, Pennsylvania.

Cleveland Amory

We've had strays at the office, and had strays go through my house on to another home, but I never had one that was all mine before Polar Bear, who I wrote about in *The Cat Who Came for Christmas*. We probably do more hands-on rescue here at the Fund for Animals than any other society. Polar Bear, this particular one, was a real individual, and so it was kind of strange, but fitting, for me to be alone there Christmas Eve when he came by. It's a rather simple story about a fellow who always had dogs and suddenly gets a cat. We're an odd couple, a curmudgeonly bachelor and a grumpy cat, sort of a test of wills. Of course, he wins ninety-nine percent of the battles, but I never admit it. That's why I'm happy and he's happy.

I've had him since 1978. He's very protective toward me, and amazingly possessive of who's doing what and why are they there and how long are they going to stay. He sits on a corner at the foot of the bed and guards. He's gotten more philosophical toward people than he was in the book. Now, when one person comes in to play chess, he doesn't move away. He knows we're going to play chess and it's going to be boring.

I've gone into the kitchen after hearing crashing sounds, after he's knocked something over while looking for something he wants, and I come in and he has this look on his face that says, "We've absolutely got to catch the perpetrator here." He's such a little phony, and I love that quality about him.

If a cat gets tired of you working on a particular thing, they just sit on top of it for awhile. I think all of the non-cat people think we're nuts. I think we're a special breed, cat people. We're not better than anybody else, we're just different. I think it's difficult for a dog person to understand us.

This difference, I used to think, could be attributed to the old days, when men liked dogs and women liked cats. Men wanted something that would come when it was called, would take a walk on a leash, would sit at his feet in the evening, and would not have anarchy in the household. And women always admired the independence of a cat, and that was in the days when they had so little of it, and now I think they have much too much of it.

I like to match my wits against his, and I kind of know that I come unarmed and that he's going to win, but I still like to try. I think cats have a huge sense of humor. They love it when you say, "No, No, No," and they stop doing something, but then at the last minute, they push it off the edge of the desk and cause a commotion, and then watch your reaction. I think they absolutely adore that, fooling people.

I don't think I can say that there's anything I don't like about cats because Polar Star just came into the room here as we're talking. I honestly don't think there is anything I dislike about them. I think we all wish they could live a little longer. They say seven years for us is one year for them, which I think is just plain untrue. It's ridiculous to think that a two-year-old cat is like a fourteen-year-old kid. A cat is much more mature. The best chart I've found gives two cat years twenty-seven human years, and three cat years, thirty-one human. A four-year-old cat is like a forty-one-year-old person. It varies a lot. I feel the seven-to-one ratio is ridiculous. For one thing, there are cats who live to age thirty; what the hell are you going to do about that? Call them 210? My vet considers Polar Bear, who is 14, the equivalent of 76, and says next year he'll be like 82. I think that's a little much. I don't think Polar Bear seems seventy-six, more like a person in his late sixties. It's very complicated, and depends on how healthy they are. Just because so many cats don't seem to need much help, people ignore taking them to the vet because they hate it so much. It's ruined my romance life because Polar Bear thinks every girl who comes in could potentially be a vet and stick him. It's ruined my chances of anything but bachelorhood. It's a message I'd like to leave—do not ignore it. You think you know everything about your cat, but very few people know about the health of a cat.

I think he knows when I'm starting a long writing project, and he does not like it. He figures it's going to be like a long chess game, stupid and boring, and in the end it's going to cause more trouble for him. I write longhand in pen. I did write the first book on a typewriter, but he gets in the way awful with a typewriter. I don't like anything to be too difficult at first. I like to just put it down like you would in a secret letter to somebody, and I get to look at it for the first time after it's typed. The office is just a hotbed of computerese; I don't understand it; I can't operate a venetian blind. Neither do I want to; I want a very nice ballpoint Mont Blanc pen in the hope that he doesn't chew it, which of course he has, but I think it is a lot easier way to sit down and write.

One story I left out of the book on purpose was: Once, I opened the door and somebody came in and Polar Bear went flying out the apartment door. I picked up the newspaper, rolled it up, and smacked him with it the way you do with a dog, just to teach him he couldn't go out because it's so damned dangerous. The elevator doors open, he goes inside, down he goes to the ground floor, next thing you know he's out on the street. But the look he gave me when I had smacked him, I couldn't ever stand that look again. It was like, "You're my friend and why did you do that?" In the first place, punishing a cat doesn't work. After that, I never did again.

I have one more cat book coming out in the fall of 1993, and then that's it.

Cleveland Amory is the founder of the Fund for Animals and the author of *The Cat Who Came for Christmas* and *The Cat and the Curmudgeon*. He lives in New York City.

Tamara Asseyev

In 1978, before we had an embassy there, I was invited by the Chinese government to go to China as part of America's first motion picture industry delegation to that country. On the trip, I met the director Tony Richardson, and we became very good friends. As it turned out, Tony lived across the street from me in Los

Angeles, but we hadn't met each other before. When we came home, I found out that my old black alley cat had died. I was heartbroken.

That Christmas, at six o'clock in the morning, my doorbell rang. It was Tony, with one of his daughters carrying a brown paper sack. They came over to wish me Merry Christmas. All of a sudden, the paper sack meowed. I opened it up and it was the most perfect little Abyssinian. I named her China. That's how I got started with Abyssinian cats. And I started to breed them, so I've always had an Abyssinian ever since then, at least a couple of them, and now, in addition to the Abyssinians, I have two Somalias, which are long-haired Abyssinians.

My cat Mao, who I bred, is a big male Abyssinian who was the role model for my book *Always Kiss with Your Whiskers*. I came home from a date one night, and was sitting on the bed. This man was really a creep, and Mao was sitting on the bed next to me, and he said, "You know, why do you go out with that jerk?" And I realized that he was savvier than I was in ways of love. I was originally going to produce a television series about a savvy talking cat who gives advice on love and business to her single mistress, but we decided to do it as a book first, then as a television series. In fact, I'm talking with the major networks about it now.

Mao's my number one cat. I've always been a cat person; I love cats. I live with cats and I'm a single lady, and I'm quite content living with my sweet cats. I have a weekend house, and occasionally I bring them back and forth with me, so they're really part of my life. And I have a cat-keeper when I go on location who takes care of them and who gives me reports on my cats.

I am a guest in my cats' home. They choose where they eat and sleep. I have all three on different diets, so they have to eat in different rooms.

Mao weighs almost fifteen pounds, and should be on a diet. The other two are beautiful Somalias named Jade and China, and weigh seven pounds each. This China is my second China. I also had an Abyssinian named Ming. I give them the same names over and over. China Number One was the cat that Tony gave me, who was Mao's mother. Then she died and I got Ming. Ming had kittens before she died, so when I got my Somalias, I named one China.

I have a house up in Santa Barbara, and there are always cats around; they know I like them. I think like a cat, and I'm very independent like a cat. They're beautiful to look at, ornamental, and affectionate, but they're also self-reliant. I love cats.

There are cat people and dog people, and I just tend to like cat people better. It certainly affects anyone I date. If they're allergic to cats, they're totally out of my life. My cats come first. I'm allergic to dogs, so a dog-lover has no future with me.

Tamara

Asseyev

Tamara Asseyev is a television and movie producer and writer living in Los Angeles. She produced the Oscar-winning film *Norma Rae*. She coauthored the book *Always Kiss with Your Whiskers: Love Advice from My Cat* with Liz Nickles and Bonnie Timmons.

Lilian Jackson Braun

I've always had Siamese, and the heroes of my books are a pair of Siamese called Koko and Yum Yum. I never had a pet until I was an adult with an apartment of my own. I was given a Siamese kitten in the late 1950s, and from then on I was smitten with Siamese cats.

I did have a real Koko and a real Yum Yum at one time. In a way, it was the character of these cats that inspired the cats in the book—although it was a previous Koko who fell out of a tenth-floor window and was killed. I was so upset about it that I wrote a short story about crime and retribution involving a cat and a mystery, which led to the writing of a novel. By that time I had the second Koko, called Koko the Great, because he was remarkably intelligent and mysterious. His littermate was named Yum Yum, a little female. He lived to be eighteen, and she to fifteen.

Then I had Yum Yum Number Two, who turned out to be a holy terror. Then I had another male Siamese named Pooh-Bah; he was a real character. Now I have Koko the Third, a real southern gentleman. The female cat I have now is named Pitti Sing. All my cats are named after characters in Gilbert and Sullivan's opera *The Mikado*.

Their naming depends on their traits. When Pooh-Bah succeeded Koko the Great, I could tell that he was no Koko. He was not going to be psychic, and he had a very quirky personality. Koko is psychic. Yum Yum has a lot of female wiles; she can get her own way just by being charming.

Cats, of course, are very inventive, and they're always coming up with new habits and new tricks that give me an idea. They really inspire my books because in plotting a novel, I don't start with a murder. I start with something a cat can do to uncover a clue. For example, Koko the Great used to rub his jaw against the light switch, and that inspired *The Cat Who Turned On and Off*. Another cat used to grab a letter in his teeth and drag it around. That inspired *The Cat Who Played Post Office*. I've had cats for thirty-five years, and they still think of new things to do that I can use in a book.

Cats are beautiful. Siamese, especially, are like living sculpture. They're mysterious; they jog my imagination. They're very independent, and I admire that, being rather independent myself. They're unpredictable, which makes them constantly interesting. They're intelligent, more so than humans sometimes think. The tongue-in-cheek premise in my books is that cats are smarter than people, or at least smarter than journalists, and having been a journalist, I can say that with impunity. They're perverse. They give the impression that they know more than you do, which is intriguing, and sometimes disconcerting. We build our lives around them.

When my first book was published, I was writing for the *Detroit Free Press,* and a lot of attention was paid to the book. There was an autograph party in a downtown bookstore, and they asked if I would bring Koko. I had a double-size exhibition coop I used when we gave parties at home, just so Koko wouldn't get stepped on. So I took Koko in the coop, his litter box, and a dish of water, and set it up in the bookstore. I was there for two hours and he spent the entire time sitting in his litter box with his back to the public. It was not a great success.

Then I took him on a radio show, and he bit the microphone. Then I was asked to take him on a TV show and he insisted on showing his rear end to the camera; he would not turn around. I call that perverse. He had his own ideas about publicity.

When Koko the Great was young, he convinced me he could talk. I was in the kitchen and I heard a suspicious noise in the living room, and I said, "Where are you, Koko?" He said, "Yow!" And I said, "What are you doing, Koko?" He said, "Yow!" I said, "Are you scratching the wing chair?" He said, "Uh-uh."

I would love to have forty-seven cats—one of each breed—but it wouldn't be practical. I'd have a Maine coon cat, an Abyssinian, a Himalayan, and all the others. But two Siamese keep us pretty busy.

Lilian Jackson Braun is the author of the best-selling mystery series, *The Cat Who . . .* She lives in Columbus, North Carolina.

Helen Gurley Brown

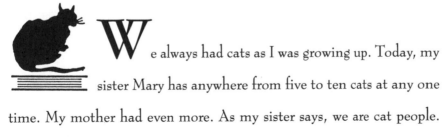

e always had cats as I was growing up. Today, my sister Mary has anywhere from five to ten cats at any one time. My mother had even more. As my sister says, we are cat people.

After I moved away from home I had a wonderful Siamese kitty, and he lived for four years. Much later, when I married David, we got one kitty, Samantha, and so that she would have a companion, acquired Gregory. Both were Siamese. They did all of the things cats *do* . . . bringing in field mice, small birds, lizards. In our old Spanish house in Pacific Palisades we had a little door in the kitchen a milkman could put the milk through. The day of the milkman had long gone, but the cats jumped through the door with their *mice*, and once Samantha brought in a really *big* bird. You know how cats are, bringing home things to Mommy to show her how smart and clever they are. I took the bird away and Samantha had a *hissy*!

They were wonderful cats. Samantha was in love with me. She spent a great deal of time on my stomach; always managed to get me into a prone position. Once I was lying down trying to read, she'd push my glasses off.

Samantha lived to be eighteen and Gregory to twelve. The last time I saw Samantha, we had just gotten back from the Cannes Film Festival. She had been going downhill over the last several months— couldn't jump up onto the radiator or on top of the refrigerator anymore. She waited for us to come home before she passed away. It's as if she needed to see us one more time. It took David (my husband) a long, long time to get over her, although I always thought of her as my cat. It seems ridiculous not to have cats now, but we travel a lot. I don't like to leave them alone because sometimes we're gone a week at a time and we don't have live-in help.

I never understood those scratching posts or trees. Pamela Mason, James Mason's wife, is a lovely "cat person" in Los Angeles, and she sent us a wonderful scratching tree about as big as a sycamore at the Bel Air Hotel. The cats wouldn't go near it. I don't think a cat's claws should be removed, so we had a toe-clipping session every six weeks. Once or twice I got skin instead of toenail . . . poor Samantha! Gregory was more docile.

Writers and cats (both superior breeds) are attracted to each other. Cats provide company, but not to the point that they interfere with your thought process. Some cats like to sit on the typewriter; both of mine did.

My girlfriend named Samantha; she just thought it was a pretty name. Sometimes, that's a nice thing you can do for somebody—help name a cat. David named Gregory, but we always called him Brownie. My sister gives her cats cat names such as Minnie and Fluffy, Blackie and Brownie, and Missy, always ending in y or ie. She doesn't approve of giving kitty cats human names. I don't think those of us who call cats Gregory and Samantha are doing it because we don't have children.

Cats are beautiful, smart, perverse, outrageous, funny, and satisfying. They are probably the best of all creatures. Cats first, then people, and everything else comes after that. I definitely will get another one.

Helen Gurley Brown is the editor in chief of *Cosmopolitan* magazine.

Helen

Gurley

Brown

Rosellen Brown

 I was one of many people who grew up thinking she didn't like cats. We didn't have any pets at all when I was a child.

When I got married, I told my husband we were going to get a cat. We went to the humane society and brought back a little kitten and named him Chatul, which means cat in Hebrew. We had him for seven years. He traveled with us from Boston to Mississippi, and then to New York. He was not a very distinctive cat, except that he had taught himself to pee in the toilet. I had my daughter Elana in 1970, and the day I went into labor, Chatul began to get sick. I remember being in the hospital talking with my husband over the phone, and he told me Chatul had died. I remember feeling really stupid, blubbering over this cat when people were saying, here you have this wonderful, healthy baby girl, what are you crying about?

I am absolutely certain that my daughter has some occult relation to catness, and that some transference of personality took place the weekend of the cat's death and her birth, because she's always had a terrific affinity for cats. When she was a child, she called herself TCH, The Cat Herself. Cats follow her everywhere, and she's the only one who can get a cat to play with her. She's twenty-one now, and not allowed to have a cat in her apartment, but they still follow her around.

Today, we have a female black-and-white cat named Coriander, and a tortoiseshell cat named Joey. Joey's brother is what we consider a gay cat. Not only does he have a girl's name, Lylah—(it means *evening* in Hebrew; and our children named him that because he's black and white) but he is very effeminate and soulful, with gorgeous eyes that look like they're ringed with eye makeup. Lylah is just this soft-hipped kind of guy. His brother is a fierce cat and they have nothing in common. I can't believe they're from the same litter.

I have written cats into my books in a couple of places that I really love. I have a funny scene in the first page of my book *Civil Wars* in which a cat walks all over a couple while they're making love. That was a cat I had named Karen. She had great curiosity and got turned on by sex.

Cats have found their way into very emotionally loaded situations in my writing, and I have given most of my characters a cat, not a dog. I think cats are much more emotionally complicated and mysterious, and they lend themselves to much more anthropomorphizing. I never would have done that if I hadn't spent so much time thinking about them and looking at them. In that way, they've been quite important to me.

Especially now that our children are gone, I hate to turn into one of those soupy kinds of parents of cats, but there's absolutely no question that we spend a lot of time looking at them and digging each other with our elbows and saying, "Will ya look at that!" It's what you do when you don't have kids at home anymore. Cats are aesthetically more pleasing than dogs; they look like they're putting on a show just for you.

The cats gather around while I write on the couch. They love to sit on my work, and they especially love to do it when their paws are dirty. There is a certain level of perversity about them, and I believe they deliberately do this type of thing to you.

Having a number of cats is especially fun. We got two the first time we were living in New Hampshire, and ever since then it's been wonderful to have more than one—two cats are more than twice as much fun as one. There's all this movement, and when three of them jump up on the counter to be fed at one time, there's something so funny about all that seething action.

I aspire to their ineffable silence, and their capacity to be comforting. The way they lie up against you in bed, all of those things; they're full of very subtle emotional adjustments to you. Cats are very attuned. They always know when you're going away. There are a lot of ways they absolutely know what's going on.

When one of us goes away, they all come up to sleep in the bed with the one left behind. They'll do that in cold weather, anyway, but even when it's hot out, they'll comfort me when I'm by myself. They know, but why do they care? They're ultimately such mysterious little beings, and that's what I love about them. They do not disclose. They're very proud. If a cat falls off a table, it will right itself, start licking itself, and look over its shoulder at you as if to say, Of course, I meant to do that.

Rosellen Brown is the author of the novels *Before and After, Tender Mercies, Civil Wars,* and *The Autobiography of My Mother.* She lives in Houston, Texas.

Susan Brownmiller

I'm a dog person; I'm on my first cat. I'm still adjusting to the methods of communication. I mean, the cat doesn't seem to respond to things like No, and Bad Cat. I have to work around that and make the cat think it's his idea. I've had Christopher—short for Christopher Robin—for two years. A friend named Robin asked me if I would take in this stray she found at Christmastime. He has many nicknames.

He's a lot of fun. I think interspecies communication is a wonderful thing, and it's a real adventure having this cat. He's a terrible biter, a pouncer, and a hunter. I have a terrace, so he has access to the outside. If I didn't have this terrace, I wouldn't have a cat, since he needs to have places to explore and hunt. Butterflies, bees, water bugs, whatever's in season he hunts. We're twenty floors up.

He's extremely curious about the laser printer; he doesn't understand it. He can't figure out how value is created from nothing, which is a problem that most people have with what writers do anyway. He can't figure out where the paper comes from. It's a front-loading printer, so he can't see the paper. All he knows is that the paper comes out the back when the machine is on, so he keeps staring at the back to find the source of the paper. Printing out is the most traumatic part of writing if you write on a computer, so he adds an extra level of anxiety for me. There comes a time when the paw has to go onto the paper to stop the process. And that is the moment when he gets picked up and taken out of the room and the door is closed. I usually try to print when he's not around, but he can hear the sounds when he's on the neighbor's terrace and will come running.

When I'm writing, he curls up at my feet—he knows that routine. He knows where I am and he likes that. He doesn't try to get in between me and the screen, which is interesting because he usually tries to get in between me and whatever else I'm staring at.

I'm trying not to become besieged by the cat iconography, because I've noticed it seizes people. Some of my friends who are perfectly normal people go into a trance when they get a postcard with a cat on it.

I have trouble with the cat's way of thinking; the sneakiness really troubles me. The lying in wait really bothers me. He practices his pounces on me. I prefer a much more straightforward relationship. He's telling me that he could bite my face if he wanted to.

Once, I went to a PEN dinner at which everyone received a Mont Blanc pen. I put mine on my desk, but the cat must have swatted it into an open file drawer. I screamed at him, whereupon he stiffened his little shoulders and quivered as if to say, she's my human companion and I have to put up with her irrational behavior. At that moment I knew I loved him. So I went out and bought another Mont Blanc pen, which I very carefully put away. He loves to bat my cigarette lighter into oblivion, but they only cost $1.50.

Friends tease that any cat living with me will have a hard time because it will not be in charge. We had one day of grace, the day he came here, grateful for a home. After that it was, okay, now what can I do to get in charge? And he was only eight weeks old.

Having a cat has made me think a lot about genetics and the nature-versus-nurture question. I admire their self-centeredness and their survival skills. They're such a funny combination of real risk-taking and extreme caution. It seems to me that most people who get cats the way I did attribute a cat's behavioral problems to some prior terrible mistreatment or early trauma. I decided this isn't true in Christopher's case. He came from a tough set of parents.

Susan Brownmiller is the author of *Against Our Will: Men, Women and Rape, Femininity,* and *Waverly Place,* a novel.

John Casey

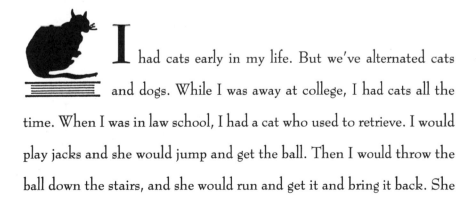 I had cats early in my life. But we've alternated cats and dogs. While I was away at college, I had cats all the time. When I was in law school, I had a cat who used to retrieve. I would play jacks and she would jump and get the ball. Then I would throw the ball down the stairs, and she would run and get it and bring it back. She

got hit by a car. I lost another cat to a girlfriend, which is often the case.

I don't think it's a good idea to have a cat unless you're going to be in one place for awhile. Dogs travel with people, and cats sort of go with the house.

My cat Bilbo now has the longest tenure of any cat I've had. We were living in Rhode Island, and my younger daughter had wanted a cat, and the older one wanted a pony. A cat seemed like a pretty cheap out. This was in the fall of '79. This cat wandered in out of an early unseasonable snowstorm, October or November, and this little runt about three to five weeks old attached itself to the older daughter with the pony already.

So, we had to get another cat for the younger daughter. I bought her a very expensive Burmese cat. I always like the way Burmese looked, but this one was an absolute moron. This is not what you expect from cats. You expect intelligence, a certain irony, and self-sufficiency. This cat went to the attic and fell down between the walls, from the third floor to the bottom floor. We heard it going mew mew, but we couldn't tell where it was. We chopped through plaster walls and finally found it. It used to wander off and couldn't find its way back, so my daughter and I would go looking for it. Finally it wandered off, never to be found again. We had it for six years.

I can write in a room with a cat, but not with a dog. I write longhand, and my cat knows to get in the way is not how to proceed in the world. The cat doesn't want to pierce your attention barrier. It's sensitive to your attention being in a globe around you, and her attention being in a globe around her. When the time is appropriate, you can sort of overlap globes briefly, but you're not going to do things you do with a dog, like hunting together. Sometimes I think I want to get a Maine coon cat, a real slugger.

A dog's attention is too much, a cat's too little, so I'm looking for something in between.

I had a cat named Petunia Blossom that used to jump up on the dining room table. She was a mutt cat, but there was a lot of Persian in her—you couldn't get your hand around her tail. Once, we had candles lit on the table, and she walked by the candles and her tail went up in flames. But she maintained her beautiful, sedate walk; she never altered her stride; she never felt anything. I grabbed her by the stump of the tail and she ran off. Charred fur came off it. She never felt a thing, but she was slightly surprised.

Somehow, cats, flowers, houseplants, and Turkish rugs all seem to go together, the house seems incomplete with any one of them missing.

I find it difficult to put animals into books without them becoming cute. I think there are cat characteristics I would give to human characters, and there's a certain eros and grace that would be nice to inject into a character. There's a bit part in the first novel I wrote called *An American Romance*. One of the things about Petunia Blossom is that she had a slight retard between being touched and responding. I found it very sexy, so I gave it to a minor character in the book named Annabelle. It's almost like playing the organ. You have to be a little ahead of it; you don't get the sound right away. You would stroke, then beat, beat, then Ohhhh. It transferred very well.

I think that people who have cats give better backrubs. Cats very quickly instruct you how they want to be petted. Here's something we could all learn from cats, because cats never pay you back in backrubs. And yet people continue to rub them. If we could only get the knack of how they do it. I think it's because they have such an articulate response with their bodies that it encourages the backrubber to go on and on.

I thing poetry suits cats better than prose. Writing a novel is like trying to turn an ocean liner. In poetry you can swivel much more easily. With a plot turn in a novel, you have to plan the bow thrust and give the crew plenty of warning. A poem is more like a kayak, it can turn on a dime. For some reason, that's what's attractive about cats, a kind of silky swivel in their attention.

John Casey is the author of *An American Romance, Testimony and Demeanor,* and *Spartina,* which won the National Book Award in 1989. He teaches English at the University of Virginia in Charlottesville.

Jill Ker Conway

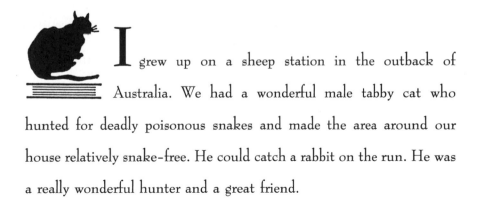I grew up on a sheep station in the outback of Australia. We had a wonderful male tabby cat who hunted for deadly poisonous snakes and made the area around our house relatively snake-free. He could catch a rabbit on the run. He was a really wonderful hunter and a great friend.

The cats I have now are purebred Maine coon cats. Tessa and Camilla are sisters and are about four years old. They're great assistants in writing. I always get up very early in the morning to write, and they're both around. One of them often gets in the out box while the other one's on my lap; they take turns. But I've never written about cats in my work; they really haven't given me permission yet.

I think that it's the companionability of cats that particularly appeals to writers. There are very few other animals who will just come and be with you, and be a companion to you. As soon as I sit down at my desk, they're there.

Certainly, cats have always recognized a kindred spirit in me. They're such beautiful creatures; they radiate such well-being and grace and relaxation that they always calm me down.

They are extremely interested in everything that's going on about the house. They inspect people and find out who is really acceptable and who is not. They always check out the visitors who are staying in the guest room, and Tessa, in particular, is the one who likes to dominate people. She can take a flying leap from the ground and land on your shoulder.

The cat I had before Tessa and Camilla was named Kameha Meha, after the last king of the Hawaiian islands. He was a real hunter and was extremely active in the fall when the field mice would come into our house in the country. Of course, he would always bring everything into the bedroom. One night I tired of this, so I put him out and shut the door and refused to admit him. When we got up in the morning there were four mice laid out parallel in descending order of size right outside the bedroom door. He left a very splendid tribute.

I think it's quite impossible for a human to think like a cat. They are such distinctive beings; they follow their own logic and nothing sways them. But I think cats are wonderfully sensitive to people's moods; they always know just before you do how you're feeling.

I like their humor and their playfulness and their affection and their wonderful regal composure. Kam used to go into a cupboard in my study and tear up old income tax returns. He was a personal shredder. There's nothing I don't like about cats.

All our cats like music. Camilla likes Gilbert and Sullivan and Tessa has a great taste for Mozart. She sits in front of the speaker and lets the vibration go right through her head.

My cats are a constant source of amazement to me because of the ingenuity they display in getting the world organized the way they want it. While I've always been dotty about cats, it's been fascinating for me to notice how all of the people who regularly spend time in my house—my secretary, cook, and housekeeper—have been totally converted into servants of these two creatures. And I think that without ever really dominating people, the cats have everyone reorganize their lives for them.

Jill Ker
Conway

Jill Ker Conway is a historian, writer and educator who studies the history of women, the history of education, and the history of environmental movements. Her most recent book is *The Road from Coorain*. She is married to John Conway (also a cat-lover) and lives in Boston and in Western Massachusetts.

© DEPAOLA '92

Tomie dePaola

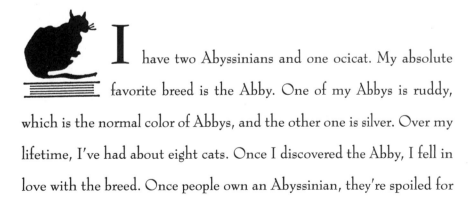 I have two Abyssinians and one ocicat. My absolute favorite breed is the Abby. One of my Abbys is ruddy, which is the normal color of Abbys, and the other one is silver. Over my lifetime, I've had about eight cats. Once I discovered the Abby, I fell in love with the breed. Once people own an Abyssinian, they're spoiled for

life because they're very special. They're beautiful, very affectionate and friendly, and they don't meow—just a little ee.

The ocicat is named Bomba. The ruddy Abby is named Foshay, because he came from a breeder in New Hope, Minnesota, and there's a tower in Minneapolis named the Foshay Tower, which was the highest skyscraper in the early days of the city. The silver Abby is also from the New Hope breeder, and I named him Dayton, because I once worked for Dayton's department store designing their flower show.

I had another Abby who was with me for seventeen years. I named him Satie, because one of my favorite pieces is *Gymnopedie*, by Erik Satie. Whenever I put that piece on, he would lie right in front of the speakers with his ears tucked back. I'm positive he was Erik Satie reincarnated. I used him in a book I did last spring called *Bonjour, Mr. Satie*. I was convinced he was very erudite and the minute I left would call all of his friends and have parties or travel. He just had that all-knowing, wise look about his eyes.

I didn't dare write the story about Satie until he was gone. I'm sure he would have insisted on going off on autograph tours. I did put him in drawings. He was amazing. He'd walk into the middle of a room and sit there so that everyone would notice him. He was very aloof-looking.

I've always tried to keep the cats out of my studio because there's just too much stuff—paintbrushes and so on. Satie was very good about things, but if he thought I'd been working too long he'd come and sit right on top of the artwork.

I think once you get hooked on cats, it's difficult not to have a cat in your life. I do think cats are psychic—they pick up things very quickly. They know when I'm going away, even if I keep the door shut while I'm packing. Once, I made the mistake of putting the suitcases out too early for a trip. I was leaving at five in the morning, and at three a.m., two of them decided to beat up on each other.

What I find fascinating with three cats is that they set up different relationships daily. Sometimes the three of them will be very friendly; then it's two versus one in various combinations. I'll see three curled up together, or two curled up together, or all three separated. It's as though they have new rules every single day.

I'm a firm believer that you can train cats, and I've done that with my cats. The one thing that's really impossible is teaching them not to get up on counters. They won't get on the counters while I'm home, but

I have white tile counters and I'll come back into the house and find little pawprints all over. They think, a-ha, let's get on the counters now that he's gone.

With Dayton, if he doesn't get enough attention, he throws up. I've taken him to the vet, and there's nothing physically wrong with him. At six in the morning I'll hear these sounds and wonder, god, where'd he do it now? I tell people to please hang up their coats—don't leave them lying on a chair. One time, I had white carpeting laid down in one room and two seconds after it was finished, Dayton went in and threw up right in the middle of it.

I think my cats have had a lot of influence in my artwork, but not so much my writing. You live with a cat like the Abby, and you have a good moving design around you all the time. I'm always so aware of the ways my cats will arrange themselves in the perfect way, and they never sit on anything that doesn't complement their color. I am absolutely serious. I'm sure I could go in and set down five pillows and they would pick the one that they would look the best on. And, of course, it works out quite well because they're all different colors. Quite often, Foshay and Bomba will be stretched out completely on this gray radiator downstairs in the basement, looking like they're melting into one big pattern of fur, eyes, and whiskers.

I think that just having this beautiful living object around really does keep me visually aware. My dogs, on the other hand, are a totally different story. They're the epitome of comfort. Cats always arrange themselves; dogs just plop.

It sure would be a cushy life to come back as an indoor cat.

Tomie dePaola writes and illustrates children's books. He lives in New London, New Hampshire.

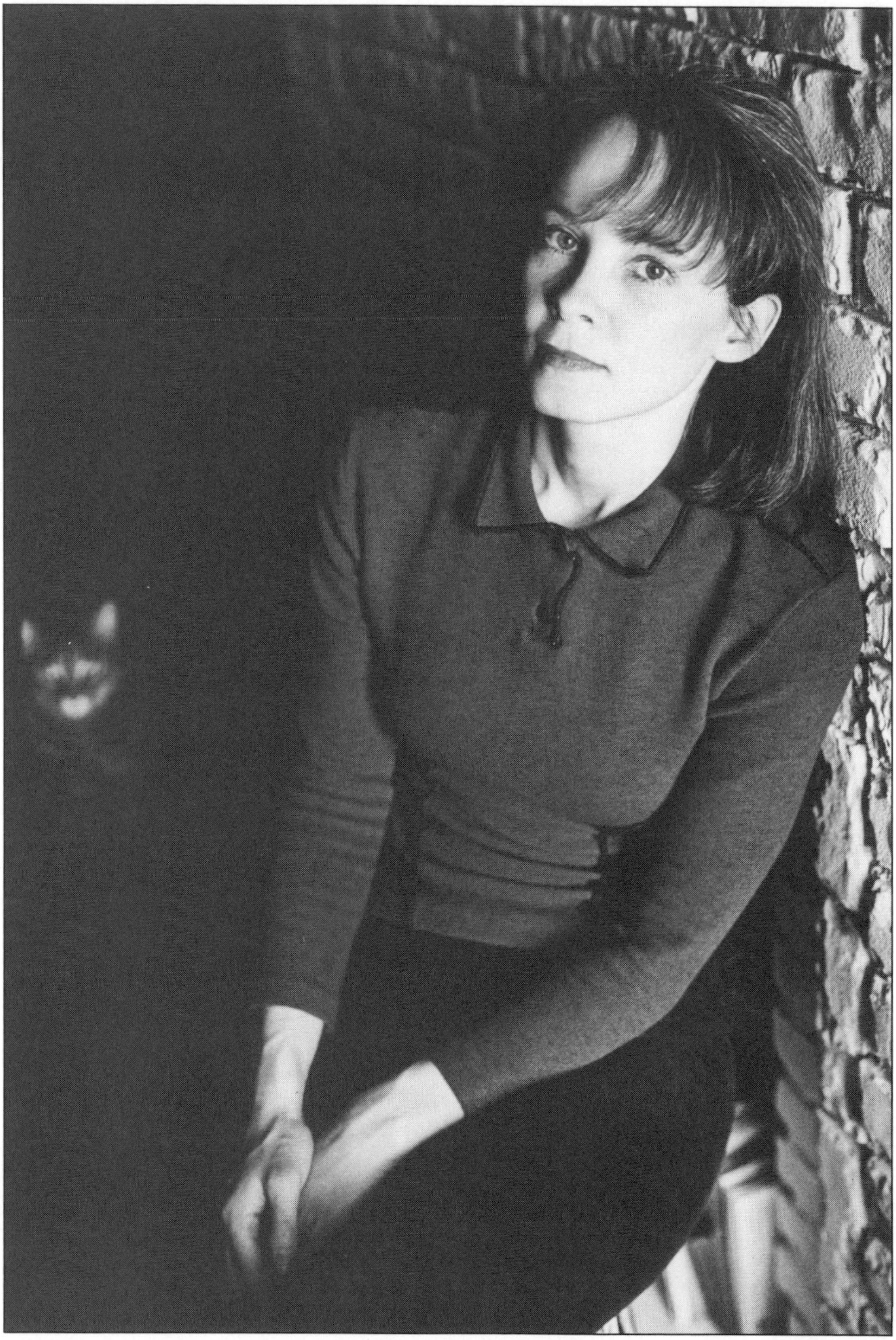

Mary Gaitskill

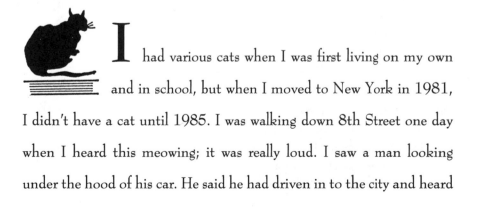 I had various cats when I was first living on my own and in school, but when I moved to New York in 1981, I didn't have a cat until 1985. I was walking down 8th Street one day when I heard this meowing; it was really loud. I saw a man looking under the hood of his car. He said he had driven in to the city and heard

a constant meowing. I stopped on the street to look along with other people and saw a black-and-gray tabby kitten under the hood. He pulled her out. She was very warm, the end of her tail looked like it had been chewed up a little, and the pads of her feet were really hot. I ended up holding the cat, even though I thought I wouldn't keep her because I had a tiny apartment at the time. So I took her to the art school on 8th Street. First they said they couldn't take her, but then they said, "Maybe we could; she is very pretty." But when they took her out of my arms, I reflexively reached out for her, and someone said, wisely, "Let her hold her for awhile." And I said, "Maybe I'll take her home," even though I intended to give her away. I got very attached to her and kept her and named her Suki.

I tried to adopt a second cat named Spike, but I couldn't get anything done because Suki and Spike fought all the time. I even dreamed about it; it was a nightmare. People kept telling me to calm down, it's just cats, but you invest in them such drama. I couldn't work at all.

There's a certain tenor to our life that is good for both of us. The tone of our life in the house is almost boring, as I live in a very quiet, hermetic way. I don't know how cats think; I don't know what she thinks I'm doing with this pen and paper, but I think she's aware of the vibrational quality of the experience. It's possible that she likes the feeling of intensity there, but it's low key and doesn't have a lot of jagged edges. She has a grounding effect on me. Animals have a kind of fundamental and uncomplicated connectedness to life that people typically don't have and that I like to be reminded of.

My sisters and I are all cat nuts, and we don't have children. We were home for Christmas and were telling long, elaborate stories about the cats and what they've done, and my mother expressed her bewilderment and consternation, and asked why we find this so endlessly interesting?

As for writers and cats, there's something very internal about cats. Cats like to go out, but they do so in a stealthy manner. Writers, even though they might be sociable and extroverted, have to draw on their subterranean, internal qualities, and since the cat embodies these qualities, it may help the writer invoke them. If a writer mentions a cat in a story, it brings this animal presence into the book in a way a human can't—even if it's just a cat walking across a floor.

Once, when I had the flu, all I could manage to do was to go to the bathroom and feed the cat. The entire time I was sick, Suki stayed by my side, instead of charging around and demanding that I play, which is what she usually did. When my fever broke, she sniffed me, realized I was feeling better, and immediately jumped onto the dresser and started batting stuff around.

One time when I went to visit my parents, I used the visit as a Fresh Air Fund for Suki. I thought it would be good for her to get outside and be in a big house. She was two years old and spayed and thus, I thought, unlikely to wander. There was a ten-foot-high fence around the yard, so I thought she was pretty safe. The first few outings she stayed in the yard, but eventually went right over the fence and disappeared. I went around the block, calling her. I put up "Lost Cat" notices around the neighborhood, but nobody found her. One night, when I was in the front of the house typing, I suddenly had the feeling that she was out in the backyard, even though I could not possibly have heard her. I went out there and called but she wasn't there. I went back in, but I was still convinced she was out there calling me, so I went back out and she answered me. I located her on the other side of the fence.

I don't have a favorite literary cat, nor do I connect my cat's presence with my writing in any direct way. It's almost impossible to write about them without having them appear like a greeting-card cat. My relationship with Suki takes place in a different realm from the complicated human mental and emotional thing that happens when you write. As an animal she's directly linked to a fierce tenacity that's integral to life at its most basic level. As a cat she brings that forward with innate refinement and grace. Her presence is good for me in that it brings me all of these qualities, and is therefore beneficial to my writing in an indirect way.

Mary Gaitskill is the author of *Bad Behavior*, a short-story collection, and a novel, *Two Girls Fat and Thin*.

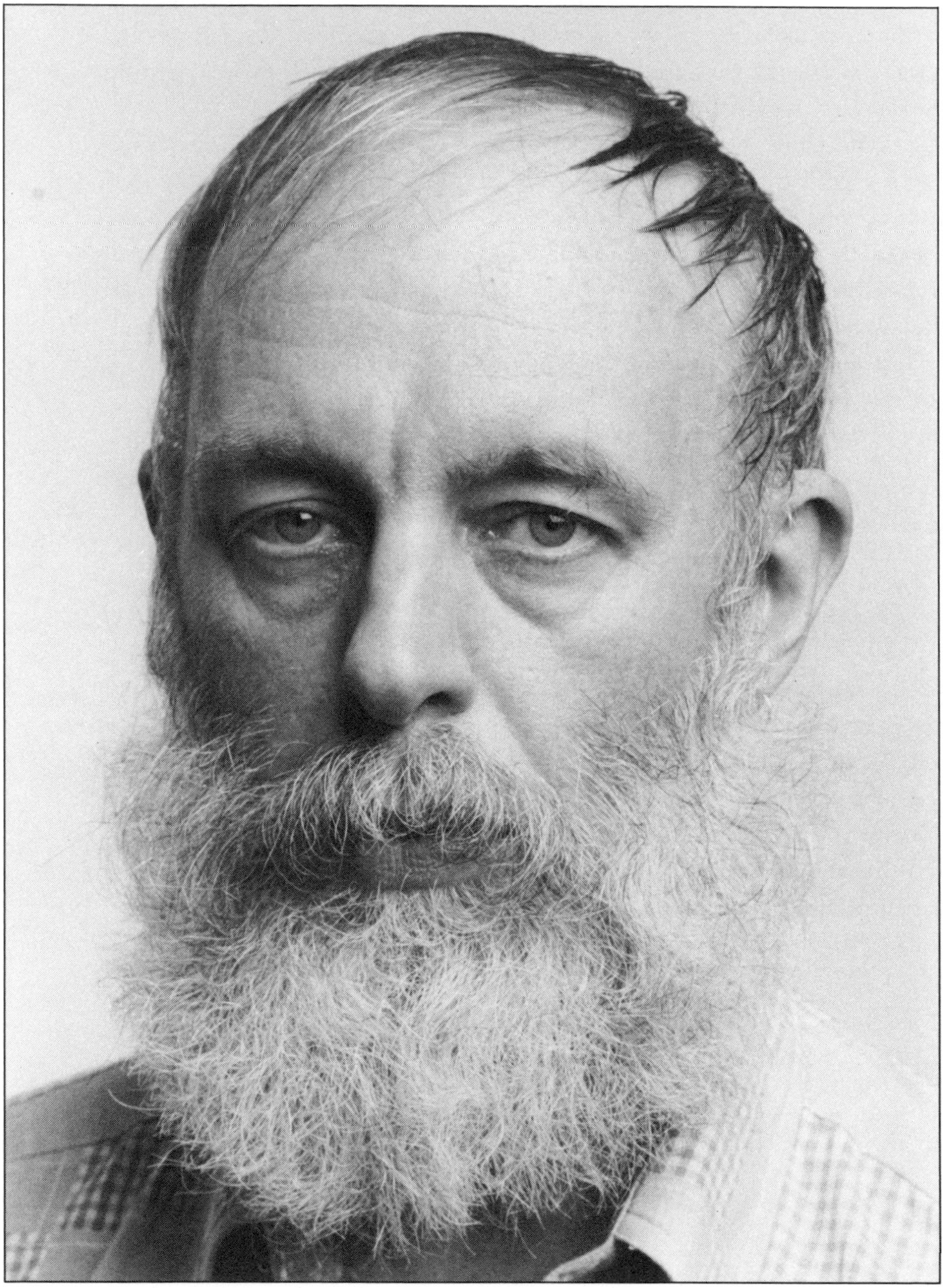

Edward Gorey

I've always had at least one cat. At the moment I have seven. I love them dearly, but I sometimes feel they're largely an irritation, and I seem to spend most of my time screaming at them not to do things, not that it does any good. Whenever I read about people who train their cats not to scratch the furniture, I think,

"Oh, they're very lucky, the cat just doesn't want to." In my experience, no matter how many times I scream at them not to do a particular thing, they still go ahead and do it.

Occasionally, due to my own carelessness, they'll ruin a drawing because I'll leave a bottle of ink open and they'll walk across the paper. I can't leave a pen lying on the board because even if Thomas is at the other end of the house, he'll know when I walk away from the drawing board even for a split second and will rush in to play with the pens. I'm missing about half a dozen pens.

My two oldest cats are ginger tabs named Billy and Charley. The next oldest ones are named George and Weedon; then I have a brother and two sisters named Thomas, Alice and Jane. They all get along very well together, and they tend to sleep in one great big lump. There are a couple that sit up on my drawing board while I'm working. They're all such good friends. They almost never hiss at each other, but maybe once or twice a day one will hit another one where I can't see them and I'll yell, "Stop it! Stop it! Stop it!"

When I lived in New York for part of the year in a one-room apartment, I felt three cats was as much as I could handle, although I did end up with six for a year or two. Let's put it this way, I will probably have acquired a few more by the time this book comes out.

I have a couple of cousins who live near me, and occasionally they go off to the ASPCA to get a cat, and I always ask *why*? Good God, I live in mortal terror of finding more outside, or somebody turning up on my doorstep. With one exception, all of my cats have been strays. People come and say, "If you don't take this cat, it's going to the pound." God knows I do that myself. When I've come across a stray and I can't have any more cats, I blackmail people. You know: "You owe me one, here's a cat, take it."

They can be the most godawful nuisances. The minute I go to bed, Charlie comes up and claws me because he wants to sleep right in the crook of my arm and his nose in my face. Nothing I can do will stop him. If I put the bedclothes over my head, he'll just sit there clawing at the bedclothes until I finally give up. And, of course, once he's there, he wants to leave after five minutes. So, in the middle of the night he leaves, and then he wants to come back in and he'll start clawing at the bedclothes again. Jane and Thomas both like coming under the bedclothes briefly, but then they slither out again, and they only want to go between *part* of the bedclothes, under one bedspread and one blanket. Then there's another who wants to go under only *two* blankets. I have to allow them to weasel their way in, so when all seven have decided they want to sleep in the bed, it's definitely difficult to turn over.

Cats are pretty independent and they go about leading their own lives in the house. I wouldn't live without them. In one way they're very demanding, but in another way they're not demanding at all. My cats have influenced me a great deal, but I can say I have no idea what they're thinking about. None of my cats ever seem to do anything wonderfully picturesque, or wonderfully clever, and nobody's been abysmally stupid, either.

We all sit on the couch and watch television together. They have an annoying tendency to stand up and get in the way of the TV and block the view just at the crucial moment. We watch TV upstairs in a room with skylights and sometimes they'll all suddenly look up at once, and I have no idea what they're seeing. The only time I get spooked living alone is when the cats get spooked. When I lived in New York, there were some times when the cats would suddenly get very twitchy and I'd think, there's something going on, and I could never figure out what it was. I don't know if they're particularly psychic, but they're obviously attuned to something we're not.

One thing I've never understood is showing cats or breeding cats. I came across a cat book a couple of years ago and was horrified to see all of the monster races of cats that are out there. I've always had domestic shorthairs; Abyssinian is the only exotic I've ever had at all. They're still wild animals, despite the fact they're living in the house. What appeals to me is that strange combination of cozy, cuddly, you-can-tickle-their-tummies-and-they'll-lick-your-ear—and there's obviously something about them that's utterly remote from people, and I find that sort of nice.

Edward Gorey, writer and illustrator, lives on Cape Cod.

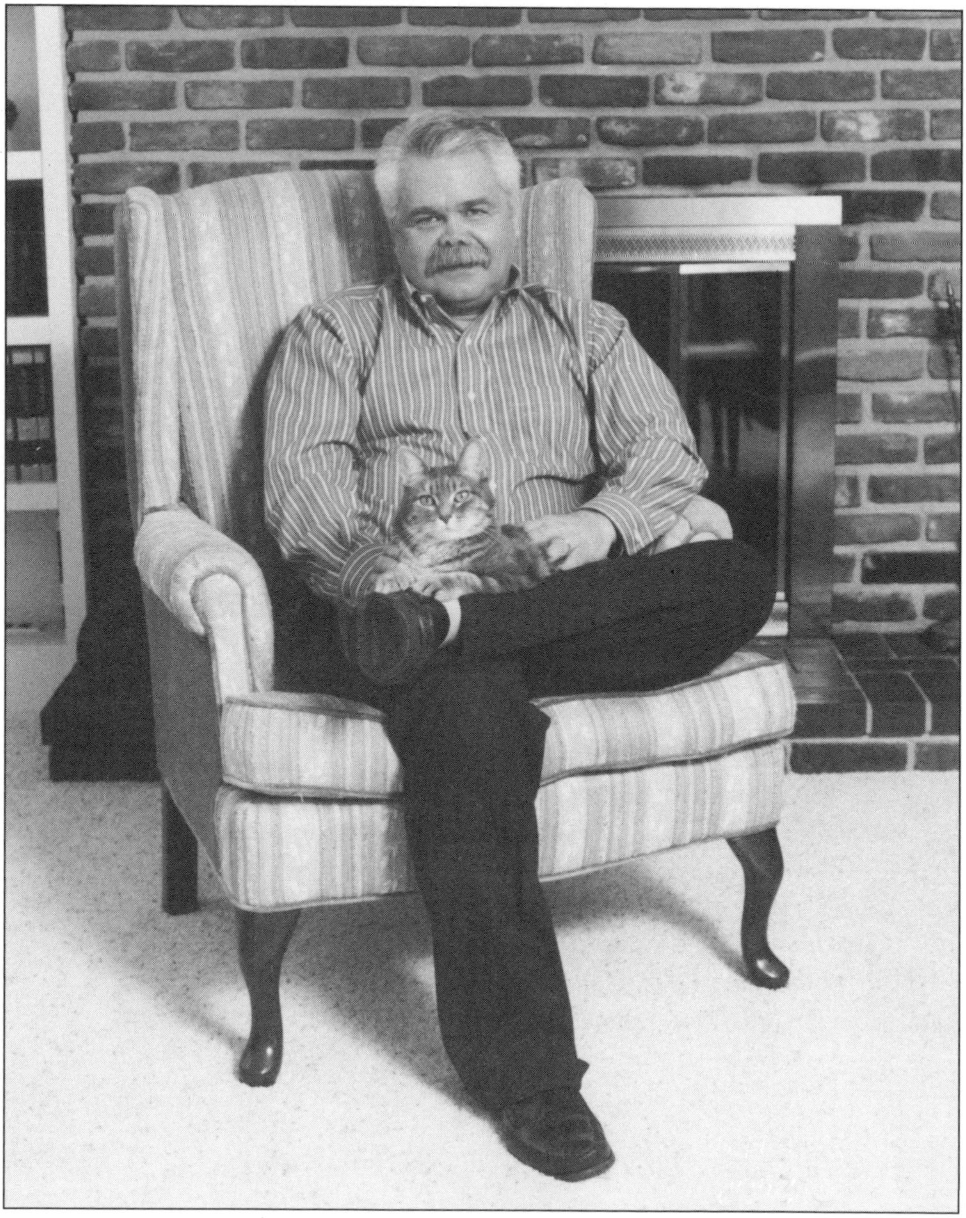

Ed Gorman

I didn't always like cats. I suppose this had something to do with my own self-image. Cats were for men destined to be poets, whereas dogs were more for regular guys. I wanted—how I wanted—to be a regular guy.

This went on well into my thirties when, one drab spring morning,

I awoke knowing neither my name nor my present whereabouts, and found next to me a woman who spoke a language other than English. Years later, this would all be funny in a grisly sort of way, but that morning it was not funny at all. My life was completely out of control. I was an alcoholic.

That afternoon, without a word to anybody (the nice thing about being divorced and a bad father is that your time is completely your own) I went up on the gorgeous rolling Iowa River, where for two weeks I stayed in a cabin and attempted to detoxify myself. I put several fists through several walls, I cried enough tears to prove I was no regular guy at all, and I made a pact with myself to never take another drink of alcohol.

Seventeen years later, I've managed to keep this pledge and I've done it, I think, with the help of two cats in particular.

When I got back from the Iowa River, I called my nine-year-old son Joe and told him where I'd been and why I'd been there and how afraid I was of the days ahead. He said it sounded as if I needed some steady companionship, that both he and his mother worried about me and how I spent so much time alone.

The next afternoon—windows open to soft spring, me banging away at the free-lance ad copy I wrote for a living in those glum days—somebody knocked at my door. When I opened it there stood Joe with a tiny kitten, followed by his mother bearing a litter box and litter. They set everything up and then let the kitty loose to prowl. I couldn't find it in myself to tell them I didn't much care for kitties.

Weeks went by and Ayesha (so named for H. Rider Haggard's eternal goddess) became my best friend. Those long nights when I wanted a drink, she sat in my lap and watched TV. Those long days when I wrote stories for minor literary magazines, she lay next to my typewriter and slept. She even went for rides with me in the country, liking to sit up on the dashboard and gaze on the dairy cows and beautiful horses not far from where we lived.

But she didn't grow at all and this began to trouble me. One day I took her to a veterinarian. He called me a few days later to say that Ayesha had leukemia and would be dead soon. And so it was. She began to vomit and lose weight. She went for days without being able to hold anything down. And finally, when I realized that I was keeping her alive for my sake instead of hers, I brought her to him, very much like delivering a prisoner for execution, and he took her with professional solemnity and I never saw her again, although her picture still hangs in my office.

I've never gotten over the loss of Ayesha or later, Doc, or little Eloise. They were friends and companions and soulmates. Right now, a cat named Tess is sprawled on my monitor watching me. To the right of my machine sits beautiful Tasha, and bounding over to the food bowl at the moment is Crystal, who genuinely believes that my wife Carol is her mother.

And speaking of my wife, at the time we met, she didn't like cats at all. But one day, not long after we were married, she came home from her teaching job with a small kitten in her arms and said, "Here's a new one." It was a classically striped kitty that some schoolboys had been throwing rocks at. A month later, Carol brought home a second homeless cat. She had apparently changed her mind about felines—just as I had, years earlier.

Ed Gorman, short-story writer, novelist, and editor of *Mystery Scene* and *Cat Crimes*, lives in Cedar Rapids, Iowa. *The San Diego Union* recently called him "One of today's best crime writers." Gorman's novels *A Cry of Shadows* and *The Autumn Dead* were dubbed "Among the most stylistically sophisticated detective stories I've ever read" by Dean R. Koontz.

Sue Grafton

I like cats because they're perfect. Our two current cats are Mulligan, a fourteen-and-a-half-pound black male with an attitude, and Ping, a seventeen-pound white male.

My favorite cat was a stray named DJ who started hanging out at our house. Our cats detested him, but he was very persistent, creeping in our cat door and eating all of their food. We thought he was the neighbor's cat and we complained repeatedly. The neighbor was baffled, but said he was doing what he could to keep his cat inside. Finally, we actually saw the neighbor's cat and it looked nothing at all like the cat hanging out at our house. By then, cunningly, DJ had endeared himself to me, though to no one else. He liked a lot of eye contact and a lot of body contact, too. He had a head the size of a softball, but otherwise he was an unremarkable-looking gray tabby. I was in love with him, of course. We had him neutered and got him all his shots. Then he got sick and it turned out he had feline leukemia. This was before immunization was possible. I'm still not sure whether he caught the disease from one of the cats we owned or whether they caught feline leukemia from him. At any rate, DJ died first. He developed a raging fever and in the end we had to have him put down. I held him when they injected him because I felt I owed him that. I went home and hung his cat tag on a little twig out on the oak tree that overlooked the patio. The windchimes began to tinkle and I was convinced it was DJ, saying goodbye to me. After that, within eighteen months, we lost the three other cats in the household, all to variations of leukemia, so we ended up with four tags hanging on the oak tree. It was very hard on us, but I couldn't blame DJ. This was maybe nine years ago and I still think about him whenever I hear wind chimes.

I've always been a cat person. I adopted my first cat, a female gray tabby, when I was in grade school. I rescued her from a kid in the neighborhood when I found him swinging her by the tail. I named her Beautiful. She had kittens rather quickly and my parents suggested that we take her to the pound, promising that they'd find a wonderful home for Beautiful and her babies. Some time later, we went down to the pound to get one of those Creatures That Bark (at my father's insistence), and there she was—still with her kittens, none of them placed. Talk about betrayal. I wept myself silly, but it did no good. And just to make matters worse, the Creature That Barks, which we acquired on that trip, turned out to be an awful beast with a crippled leg and a nasty disposition. This was my parent's notion of a good house pet.

I've heard there are actually writers who prefer Creatures That Bark, but I probably don't like their work. My cats have had no real influence on my work, but they certainly control my life. They demand absolute obedience from us. We have to do everything they tell us right that minute, or they bite. Actually, the two we have at the moment behave more like Creatures That Bark. I'm not sure how cats get their Earth names, but I know that in the naming of a cat you have to wait, keeping very still, until the cat lets you know what his or her name really is. Of course, there are many examples of owners who have foolishly insisted on inflicting the wrong name on a cat. These poor beasts simply have to endure the humiliation. When you meet such a cat, he or she will exchange a look with you in which you're given to understand that a terrible mistake has been made, but not by the cat. I'm very good at "hearing" what a cat's real name is. I've never met a child who had any talent whatsoever in the cat-naming department. Witness my own youthful folly in naming my first cat Beautiful. No respectable feline would ever offer that up as an Earth name. It's so pretentious.

The most expensive thing Ping ever destroyed was his own right hind leg, about a year after we got him. He was apparently hit by a car, shattering his femur or his tibia or whatever he walks on back there. We ended up taking him down to Oxnard, thirty miles south of us, to a feline orthopedic specialist who proposed surgery for $750. We were flat broke at the time, but I wasn't about to have the cat put down just because we were penniless. How dumb can you get? Money always comes along, but a good cat is forever. We charged the vet care to VISA and paid the bill off bit by bit. Overall, the cat's leg cost us about fifteen hundred dollars. I now regard him as a portable savings account. The problem is, even if you shake him, you still can't get the money out. My husband, Steve Humphrey, and I met because of our cats. Seventeen years ago, we were living in the same apartment building in West Los Angeles. He had an orange male kitten named Alonzo and I had a little long-haired tortoiseshell female named Molly Maguire. The two would play together down in the courtyard and we'd stand around like indulgent parents at a playground, chatting about their various accomplishments. Eventually those conversations developed into a romance. Cats in one form or another have always been part of our relationship. Aaawww.

I'm sure in my dotage I'll be one of those cantankerous old ladies who hold off the sheriff's department with a shotgun, saving my beloved horde of 184 cats.

Sue Grafton is the author of eleven mystery novels, nine of which feature detective Kinsey Millhone, the latest of which is *I Is for Innocent*. Her two other mysteries are *Keziah Dane* and *The Lolly Madonna War*. She lives in Santa Barbara.

68

The Cat

on My

Shoulder

Joe Haldeman

© GAY HALDEMAN

We had a Manx cat named Pete for nineteen years. She died two years ago, and I don't have a cat now because after Pete died, I didn't have the heart to get another. Her actual name was Petronia Arbitrix, named after a cat in a book I read when I was a teenager called *The Door into Summer*, by Robert

Heinlein. In the book, the cat was male and named Petronius Arbiter. It was about a guy who was so devoted to his cat that he carried it around in a basket on his bicycle. I tried that once with Pete and she was terrified.

Pete would sit on my lap and sleep for hours while I wrote, but every so often she'd reach up and hit the keyboard just to let me know she was there. She used to sit on the top of a bookcase just over my desk, and just when I least expected it, she'd jump down on the papers and scare me.

Once, I put a cat hater in a story just to see what that was like. The person was irrational and didn't like cats, and I put him in a position where he had to save a cat's life. He did it and realized he didn't dislike them quite so much.

Pete was a telepathic cat. I write very early in the morning, starting about three a.m. so that I'm not interrupted. Once, I was writing a bizarre animal scene about combat between a shark and a killer whale. Pete snuck up behind me and for no reason at all swatted me in the rear. I almost jumped over my typewriter. She never did that before and never did so again.

I think most writers like to have a pet around. I don't know if there's any difference between dog writers and cat writers, but most writers I know who have dogs also have cats. A lot of us have cats because we tend to move around, and cats are nicely portable.

Patterning a character after a cat is done so much in science fiction that it's become a cliché. I wouldn't touch it. I guess so many writers have cats that they cast around for a model for an alien creature, and they figure, a-ha, there's one right here.

I don't think cats care too much about their names. They do seem to learn their names pretty quickly. A friend of mine has a cat, and all she has to do is say wet food and the cat runs into the kitchen. She doesn't have to be talking to the cat, but that's how she gets the cat to come. They certainly can be trained to respond to simple commands. Our Pete would respond to the sound of a spoon stirring. She liked eggs, and if you did something that sounded like an egg being beaten in a cup, she'd run into the kitchen. She'd act betrayed if you gave her water or cat food instead of an egg. Of course, you shouldn't let a cat onto the dining room table, but we often let Pete sleep on the table while we ate dinner. One time, she reached out with one paw and without looking snagged a piece of pizza and dragged it back to her, thinking that if she didn't look at it we wouldn't notice that she had stolen it. That cracked us up. She had never eaten pizza before, but she decided she liked it, and ate most of it. The next time we had pizza she made it clear that's what she wanted. She was a finicky eater otherwise.

I like cats because they're both klutzy and graceful. You know when cats do something klutzy; they always look around afterward as if to say, "I meant to do that." The clumsiest thing she ever did was to jump into an open briefcase, and it closed on her. We watched the briefcase for a good fifteen minutes while she sat inside wondering what the hell had happened. Suddenly she stood up and realized she could walk out. It was as if she had discovered a new law of physics—and she looked like she had fully intended to do that.

But cats are generally graceful. It's sad when they get older and try things and don't seem to understand they can't do them anymore, such as trying a leap and not quite making it. Pete ended up with arthritis and we had to carry her around.

Pete was always an apartment cat and had never been more than twenty feet away from us. When we moved down to Florida we visited a friend's house and went for a walk with Pete. We were about a mile down the road and lost in conversation. We started walking back, and didn't realize that Pete was investigating something. Suddenly, we realized she wasn't with us, but I did see her in the distance, a little speck of a cat. I called for her, and she jumped up in the air and galloped toward the sound of my voice. She was terrified because she had never been alone. She acted weird for days after that. I think it forced her to reevaluate the universe.

Some cats tend to gravitate toward people who don't like cats; it seems they want to produce some reaction, whether affection or revulsion. Pete was very social. Whenever we had guests she would put herself in the very middle of the group so that she was approximately equidistant from everybody. I think she assumed she was the center of attention.

Joe Haldeman is a science fiction writer living in Gainesville, Florida, and Cambridge, Massachusetts. His novels include *Mindbridge* and *The Forever War,* and his short stories and poetry have appeared in *Playboy, Harper's,* and *Omni.* Haldeman has won various awards, including the Hugo, Nebula, Ditmar, and Galaxy.

The Cat

on My

Shoulder

Carolyn G. Hart

© JOHN JERNIGAN

Being a cat lover became very important to my writing. I had just started *Deadly Valentine*, the second book in my mystery series. I was only a few pages into it when I heard this frantic meowing outside. I knew it was a kitten, so I ran outside and there was this gorgeous black-and-white kitten in the middle of the street. I picked it up and a little boy on a bicycle came up and said he saw a lady throw it out of a car. We already had a big cat named Patch, and I always promised Patch that we'd never have another cat while we had her, because she was a very jealous cat.

So I tried to explain to Patch that Sophie was a foundling and would have died if we hadn't taken her in, but nothing helped. Patch spent three months under the bed; she only came out to eat, and any time I got near her, she scratched me. This part of my life became a part of the book because I already had a cat named Agatha who lives in the bookstore in the series. So in *Deadly Valentine*, Annie, the bookstore owner, finds a kitten and brings her in, and, of course, Agatha is brokenhearted. The cat's heartbreak mirrored the human despair in the novel, which was caused by a lack of love.

Of course, I named the series' cat Agatha in honor of Agatha Christie, beginning with the first book of the series, *Death on Demand*. The reason I put Agatha in the bookstore is that if I were going to have a bookstore, I'd love to have a cat in it. It's amazing how many mystery bookstores do have cats in them.

We have two cats now, and have had eleven through the years. They're named Sophie and Cat-O-Thomas, who is the most unusual cat I've ever had. He looks like a gorilla. He's all black, with this big broad face with very deep green eyes. He's enormous, but he's the most gentle cat I've ever met. Patch and Sophie just coexisted for three years. Cat-O-Thomas charmed Sophie, and they love each other. Sophie is about three, Cat-O-Thomas about one and a half. Frankly, I would take a cat over a cocktail party anytime. I think we cat people are so shameless about our cats because we're sure we're right. I'm afraid that dog people must find us terribly tiring, though.

As a mystery writer you have to be fairly crafty and perhaps a bit manipulative, and I'd certainly say that cats are manipulative. It's amazing how these little creatures can manipulate these huge, clumsy creatures. We are totally controlled by this tiny furry animal, Sophie, that does not weigh more than 5½ pounds. If they want something, they can pretty much get it, say, within the space of a minute and a half. A favorite ploy is to scratch the furniture, and of course that means, "I want to go outside right now." If I put something down for them they don't like to eat, they scratch the paper. Talk about utter contempt. There's no more effective way to say, "I'm not going to eat this."

Sophie is a very beautiful and feminine cat, but she has a very low tolerance level for frustration. She's the only cat I've ever had that bites. If she's not satisfied with whatever it is I'm doing, out come the fangs. I have scars on both arms. She only bit when she was between six months old and a year-and-a-half. But Sophie never has to bite anymore because the minute she gets a certain look on her face, I am very quick to do whatever she wants me to. She'll come in the living room if I haven't put down food that she likes and she'll take one of her fangs and lay it on my bare ankle. That's an instructive gesture. And I move.

I love the way cats love to share their trophies with you. My cats are indoor and outdoor cats. Patch was a great hunter cat, but she really wanted you to know about it. When she came to the front door and meowed in sort of a strangled fashion, you knew not to open the door unless you want to open the door to Patch and a maimed bird or mouse. Several times, she brought mice into the house to share with us. One time, she brought in a live mouse and I told her, no, honey, bring it outside. She dropped it and I got down on my hands and knees to look for it. Of course, Patch thought this was the greatest game; she was just having a wonderful time. I lost the mouse. In the middle of the night I got up to go to the bathroom. I turned on the light and a mouse skittered across the floor. I immediately closed the bathroom door, and took Patch, who was asleep at the foot of the bed, and tossed her into the bathroom and closed the door. All hell broke loose in that bathroom; there was thudding and thumping and crashing, and I heard the clothes hamper bang around. This was just sheer murder, but what was I to do? So I went back to bed, and when I got up the next morning the clothes hamper was on its side and the lid was ajar. Patch was asleep next to it. I thought, I guess she got the mouse for me, and I picked up the cat and looked in the clothes hamper and there was the mouse, sleeping. It wasn't hurt, but it started moving around frantically after I woke it up. My only excuse for what I did next was that I was still very sleepy, but I picked up Patch and put her in the clothes hamper. Suddenly, the hamper was alive. I picked it up and put it out on the front porch. I went back out there, lifted up the hamper and took out Patch. The mouse, who still wasn't injured, streaked out of the hamper and off into the bushes. Patch, by this time, was bored with the entire thing. All I could think of was that nobody is going to believe what this mouse is going to be telling them.

Carolyn G. Hart is a mystery writer living in Oklahoma City. The eight books in her series, featuring Annie Laurance and Max Darling, have over 700,000 copies in print. She has won all three major American mystery awards for traditional novels: the Agatha, the Anthony, and the Macavity. She attributes the success of her series to the covers designed by artist Cathy Deeter that have cats on them: *Design for Murder*, *Deadly Valentine*, and *Southern Ghost*.

Nicole Hollander

I was 35 when I got my first cat, actually it was two cats. For some reason I didn't go to a shelter, but I was attracted by an ad in the paper offering cats for adoption. I went to a small apartment that smelled terribly of cats. The woman who answered the door insisted that I stay in the front room while she brought the cats to me. I remember that the only furniture in the room was an upholstered love seat in shreds and an unframed photograph of the woman tacked to the wall. She had been very beautiful. She brought out two cats. I picked John first because he was very handsome and he sat in my lap so very quietly. I didn't realize at the time he was quiet because he was sick. And then I picked Harriet because she looked like a madwoman. Before I was allowed to take them home, the woman made me sign a paper promising that every room in my house would be open to them, and that I would never close a door against them. I really can't discuss whether I've ever broken my word, because although that woman must be quite old and possibly infirm, I'm sure she'd come after me.

Harriet was always quite small, a tortoise shell cat, much more clever than John, with rather a sour disposition. She died two years ago. The vet was hopeful that Harriet was too mean to die, but sadly she was mistaken. John is eighteen years old, a mellow guy. He's one of those long-haired white cats with black markings on the top of his head that make him look like he's in a barbershop quartet. John is the model for the cat in my comic strip, although I do draw other cats in the strip. You would recognize him if you saw him sitting here now. When he's in the strip Sylvia addresses him directly. She might say, "I'll give you ten thousand dollars if you get my glasses," or "As long as you're up, get me a Coke," or "I thought you were going to make lunch." Or he's sitting right on top of her typewriter, wearing a cape.

A lot of my cartoons are built around the idea that cats understand what we are saying, but deliberately refuse to respond. For instance, you're lying in bed, right on the delicious verge of sleep, and you notice that you've left the light on in the hallway. It's shining directly in your eyes and you say to your cat: "Just this once, could you please turn off the light?" It is that stare they give you in response to your plea that inspires you to make up unkind things about them.

When I first started the strip, I thought, I can't do too many cat jokes, it'll become an addiction. So I was very careful and included one only every two or three weeks. Now I have no shame, and do a cat joke once a week. One of my favorites has a cat sitting on a chair with its paw placed against the TV screen, being cured of hairballs by a television evangelist.

Cat lovers show absolutely no restraint in discussing their cats.

They can tell cat stories long after the person they're talking to has gone into a coma, whereas cats act aloof in public. It's only when they're alone with you that they feel free to show their emotions. They are quite intensely emotional creatures, really. Try bringing a new lover home with you and they will let you know quite directly how they feel.

All the cats I've ever met like to sit on paper. I do a lot of reading for my strip, and John usually has to sit on the newspaper or on my chest between me and the magazine. There's no compromise possible, and I never learn. I try to move him, but then I have to twist my body into an incredibly awkward position to read. We cat-lovers constantly make accommodations for them. I find I sleep diagonally, so John will feel comfortable. I wake up with cramped muscles and have a permanent crick in my neck.

I would say John runs my house. He sheds a lot, so I try to pick furniture with a pattern. I like to wear black clothes, and of course that's not sensible, since John's almost all white. I do try to clean up before I leave the house, but I think I need a valet. I met a friend for lunch recently, one who doesn't have a cat, and she greeted me with, "You're covered with cat hair!" How rude! A cat owner would never dream of embarrassing a fellow cat owner by pointing out that she was covered with fur, even if it was head to foot—and if she came to your house for dinner, she wouldn't blanch if there was an occasional hair in the food.

I regret that John doesn't know that he's famous. Once I dedicated a book to my other cat, to Harriet, because I felt I had neglected her in my strip. I always drew John because he was much easier to draw. He's handsome in an uncomplicated way, like a good-looking blond guy. And Harriet was very difficult to draw because of her markings. I felt bad about her because she was just this runty little thing, and John would be lying on the couch and put one paw out and hit her on the top of the head as she passed by. He was too indolent to chase her; he just waited till she happened by. And I thought, "God, poor creature. She's suffering a great deal." So I dedicated a book to her. I could only imagine how she would have felt. I drew a picture of her next to the dedication, hissing and narrow-eyed, spitting out: "Too little, too late, girl."

Nicole

Hollander

Nicole Hollander's next book is called *Everything Here is Mine, An Unhelpful Guide to Cat Behavior*. It's a book totally about cats, just the way they like it.

80

The Cat

on My

Shoulder

Elizabeth Janeway

The cats I have now are Susannah and Loki. They're both Maine coon cats. I registered Susannah in the Cat Fancy so that she could meet a Maine coon gentleman for the purpose of having some kittens. She had five charming kittens and Loki was one of them. The others went to happy homes and we still have these, the mother and one son, who are now about ten and eight-and-a-half years old.

The history of Maine coon cats intrigues me. I think they first came over with the Vikings. I went to a cat show a couple of years ago, and saw Norwegian forest cats. They looked so much like Maine coon cats that it seemed to me the Norwegian people who had encountered America, the Vikings, must have had some of those cats with them. And it's true that any ship that went anywhere in those days carried a cat to keep the rats out of the stores on board. So I think the Norwegian forest cat came over with the Vikings and stayed behind and made a good thing out of it up in Maine. We see their descendants as Maine coon cats.

I've always been a cat person. They like to sit on whatever manuscript I'm working on. Susannah likes to sit on my husband's manuscript particularly, because she's very fond of him. She's a large cat, too, and takes up a great deal of room. You have to have a desk large enough to shove her over. It's nice to have them around when I'm writing or reading, and it's very pleasant to have a companion.

Writers sit still, and cats also do a great deal of sitting still, but both species get up and move around, too. I think if you're a person who has to be contemplative and sit at your desk communing with anything from a pencil and paper to a computer, it's nice to have around another sort of being who behaves the same way.

Cats and I talk to each other when we encounter each other, at a friend's house or at the grocery. After having cats all my life I can understand what they're thinking about, in general, and get a feeling for why they don't like it in this spot, and why they prefer to be over there, but I can't say I think like a cat. I have blinking conversations with cats—always have. We sit and blink at each other, communing in that fashion.

They're so beautiful and so funny and so sweet when they come and cuddle that I don't even mind changing litter boxes. I've always had cats, from the time I was very small. A terrible flu epidemic hit the States in the early twenties. The two people who made the most trouble for my family was me and the cat, because we kept wanting to get in to see my father and hug him when he was down with the flu. It was hard to keep out the two of us, and we came in together every time the door was opened. That particular cat was named for the German grocer who gave him to us as a kitten, and he had the wonderful name of Rhum Schottel.

When my husband and I were living in Connecticut and our children were young, we had a cat who habitually climbed the house on the grape arbor outside, and came in to sleep with them by way of the third-story window. One of our cats walked through a dinner party there with the prey in his mouth still squeaking, and all I could do was get up from the dinner table, open the front door, and say, "Out." Fortunately, he went out.

Cats are very aware of what's going on, and they hate it when my husband and I go away. But is it psychic to know that if someone takes a suitcase out they're going away? I think that's just sensible.

Elizabeth Janeway lives in New York City. Her books include *Improper Behavior, Cross Sections,* and *Between Myth and Morning.* She is a past president of the Authors Guild of America, and a past vice president of PEN. She frequently writes articles and reviews books for *The New York Times, The Atlantic, Harper's,* and the *Los Angeles Times.*

Diane Johnson

Actually, we haven't had a big turnover of cats. Our most recent is Walter. He's our all-time favorite cat, no question about it. He's a mix of Persian and Siamese, a big fluffy cat we got as a kitten from the pound. He's our favorite because he plays more games than the others. He retrieves and comes when we call. He likes to be called because it gives him a chance to run, and he runs as fast as he can. We have a house that is cantilevered over the garden, so we can see him run around the garden when he's called. He races like a white blur, and I think it's the race that he really enjoys, not us calling him.

Walter is also the only cat we've allowed to sleep on our bed, which started when he was a tiny kitten, when he first came home with us, and which we've allowed to continue. He's about six years old now. We also have a rather placid Siamese cat who's about fourteen, named Pesto.

Certainly Walter runs our house. All day long, he asks to be let in and out, and because we don't have a cat door, that involves us. Like everyone's cat, he's picky about what he eats. He has us trained and we really defer to him. We argue like parents over whether he's getting too much freedom, or too much ash in his diet.

Walter knows when my husband John is coming home. He goes and waits by the door before I can hear anything. We thought, in retrospect, that he may have sensed the big earthquake we had here. We have a circular table with a skirt, and he hid under there for awhile before the earthquake, as well as for days afterward. This is also where he goes when he wants to tune out, like when little children are in the house.

In the years our cats were having kittens, which continued until we ran out of friends, we would often have six kittens and two parent cats in the house. That was one of our reasons for staying with Siamese and Burmese and Persian. The kittens would look so fancy and beautiful that people would accept them. It's not that we don't like tabbys and other kinds of cats, because we do. Alice Adams had two of our kittens.

I think that writers like cats because, like writers, a cat has a sedentary life; cats are willing to sit around with writers. And they're beautiful, and writers appreciate beauty. But I don't know if writers like them more than other people like them, because my husband is a doctor and he's madder about them than I am.

I think my cats have impeded my writing, actually, in the way that they come and sit on what I'm working on to keep me from working on it. I've used puppies in my novels, and there were a couple of dogs hanging around in my novel *Persian Nights*, but I haven't used a cat as a main character.

What I particularly like about cats is their catness and strangeness;

there's a kind of otherness about them. I don't think I think like a cat. I think cats are much more manipulative and evasive than I am.

We have a housekeeper who's Brazilian and believes in a lot of strange religions at once. She believes that she can cure you by holding up your hand and giving you rays of light from the palm of her hand, and she thinks cats are attuned to this light and respond to it. Clearly they do accept it from her. The cats I know understand her, and when she gives them the rays, they usually get better if they've been sick. They also stand still while she's focusing her powers. They must know this is an effective treatment that requires concentration.

We used to have a cat named Tennis Ball. We named him that because when he was born our dog waited about four weeks outside the kittens nest. He would spend hours there, nose in paw, just watching the kittens. Then one day we saw the dog walking around with what we thought was a tennis ball in his mouth. When we realized it was a kitten, of course we all screamed, but in fact, he was only helping the cat move the kittens. Those cats grew up to be very close to the dog; it was very strange and very sweet.

Diane Johnson is a novelist and critic whose works include *Persian Nights*, *Health & Happiness*, and *Terrorists & Novelists.* She lives in San Francisco.

Kitty Kelley

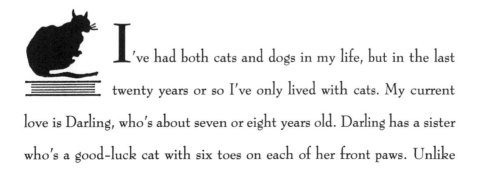 I've had both cats and dogs in my life, but in the last twenty years or so I've only lived with cats. My current love is Darling, who's about seven or eight years old. Darling has a sister who's a good-luck cat with six toes on each of her front paws. Unlike

Darling, she doesn't sit on the research files. Her name is Runtsy because she was the tiniest kitten in the litter.

When I was doing the Frank Sinatra book I had a roomful of files, and Darling's favorites were the Mafia files. He especially loved sitting on Tony "Big Tuna" Accardo. During the Nancy Reagan book research, he only sat on the President's files. (His favorite was the RR-Naps file.) He stayed away from Mrs. Reagan's files because he knew how much she hated cats.

Sometimes I prefer cats; sometimes I prefer human company. It just depends on who the human is. Some cats are more cuddly than others, just like some humans. But cats never get in the way when I write. They're not much impressed by what I produce, but they love putting their hind ends next to the warm computer.

Naturally, they run the house. They're such ancient, mysterious creatures. No, I don't think like a cat. I'm not that exotic; I'm not that sophisticated; I'm not that smart.

Some days I forget I'm living with cats and think they're really little humans in cat suits.

I'm always amazed that when I'm out with friends who are allergic or hate cats, the cats always go to them. They're so contrary. They know that *I'm* the one who wants to scoop them up and bury them in kisses.

I believe animals should be in their natural environment. I don't like kitty litter, so I've always trained my cats to meow when they need to go outside. Consequently, I've avoided the need to have kitty litter in the house.

I must say I'm a great admirer of *Washington Post* book critic, Jonathan Yardley. I can't say that about many book critics, but he seems to be a man of real intellectual integrity. I was totally convinced of this when I found out he loves cats, which more than justified my respect for him. It's easy to love a dog, because a dog follows you about adoringly. But cats are tougher—more complicated and quirky. You've got to really work to earn their affection.

I'm not too finicky about my two pure bred alley cats. They're so wonderful. One is ugly and fat and needs to be kissed everyday. Nobody would love him except for me. The other is delicate, very pretty, and acts like a princess. No, I don't like Siamese, for the same reason I don't like whippets or greyhounds: I don't like lean, mean, thin-haired, high-pitched whining animals. I love the long hair of the Angora and

Persian, but I don't like the Persian's squinched-up face. They look crabby.

My cats have been spawned from three generations of a tiger-striped tabby. Her descendants have included Angel Face, Muggsy, and Pee Wee. When my former husband and I moved to Georgetown years ago, Honeybunch disappeared after a few months. He told me that she had been killed, but I refused to believe it. I preferred to think that she had gone up the street to live at *Washington Post* publisher Katharine Graham's house, where the service was better.

I'm a big believer in the pound, and I think that most animal lovers are. I can't visit a pound, though, because I'd get too depressed. If I saw twenty cats and fifty dogs and knew that they were doomed, I'd have to call Doris Day and her rescue squad, or else take them all home myself.

I think Darling is as much my favorite as Honeybunch was. I loved that little cat because she talked in chirpy meows, chased bottle caps, and loved to watch reruns of *Born Free*. She was with me during the good times and the bad times. I remember once throwing myself on the bed and crying over something stupid, but at the time seemingly heartbreaking. She came upstairs, jumped up on the bed, and curled up beside me to be comforting. And now, every night her grandson tucks me in and then sleeps on the bed like a little sentinel. In the morning he bangs me in the face with his big furry nose and gives me the best kitty cat kiss imaginable! What a way to start the day.

Kitty Kelley is an internationally acclaimed writer whose last book, *Nancy Reagan: The Unauthorized Biography*, was the fastest selling book in America. Her previous book, *His Way: The Unauthorized Biography of Frank Sinatra*, was a number-one bestseller in the United States, England, Canada, and Australia. Her previous biographies, *Jackie Oh!* and *Elizabeth Taylor: The Last Star*, were also international bestsellers.

Rob MacGregor and
T. J. MacGregor

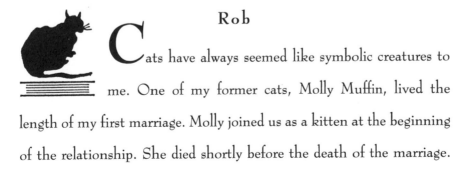

Rob

Cats have always seemed like symbolic creatures to me. One of my former cats, Molly Muffin, lived the length of my first marriage. Molly joined us as a kitten at the beginning of the relationship. She died shortly before the death of the marriage.

We got another cat, Shelly, to replace Molly, but it was too late to patch things up. I ended up with Shelly, and now ten years later she's still skittish, the product of a divorce.

No mystery novel should be without at least one cat. In my first novel, *Crystal Skull,* I use a cat as a red herring. The private investigator thinks he is stalking a killer in the upstairs bedroom of his girlfriend's house, which has been ransacked. Instead of a killer, he finds the neighbor's cat.

In the novel I'm currently writing, a mystery called *The Fifth Essence,* a cat named Two-Bits plays a minor role. Two-Bits was owned by a man who has disappeared, and the gold quarter attached to the cat's collar is a clue to what happened to him. Two-Bits, by the way, is residing at the Kitty Hotel, a cat boarding house in the neighborhood.

Until our daughter, Megan, came along, our two cats used to be like our children. Now the cats are second-class children. They've had to make some adjustments to a child in the house. Of course, so have we!

Of the fictional cats, I think Garfield is my favorite. He's something of a trickster. For instance, one day a large envelope arrived from Ballantine Books that was marked fan mail. When we opened it up, we were surprised to find that every letter was written by a child and praising Garfield. There wasn't a single letter to either of us. Ballantine had sent us the wrong envelope. But I think Garfield was behind it.

Sometimes it seems like the world is divided between the cat lovers and the cat haters. I tend to empathize more with the cat lovers. Cat haters seem to be not as sensitive as other people; they're suspicious of cats because they're so independent. I think cat haters tend to be prone to violence, too.

Once I was working at a newspaper on deadline and about mid-morning, for some reason, the image of my cat flashed across my mind. I saw it open its mouth and just howl really loudly. It was very clear in my mind, and I thought that was an odd thing to think about as I'm trying to get this story out, and I didn't think any more about it that day. Then, when I got home that night, Trish told me that that morning, all of a sudden, Shelly just let out this loud howl, probably the same time I saw it happen in my mind. I never knew why she did it, and Shelly never told me.

Trish's cat sometimes bosses her around; it swats at her when it doesn't like the cat food. I keep buying tuna and Trish keeps giving it to the cat. She has three or four different little cans of cat food open all the time just to appease Fox, and I think Fox takes advantage of it.

Cats and writers both have their own territory to protect, and independence is just something that goes along with being a cat or being a writer.

T. J.

We've got two cats, a Mutt and Jeff with distinctive personalities. Fox is a four-year-old tabby, feisty and impatient, the huntress of the family. Shelly is a chubby, eleven-year-old Persian who would probably be happier someplace colder because she has so much hair.

Rob and I have separate dens, and both cats have favorite spots in our respective areas. Shelly prefers a corner, someplace cool and shadowed where she can curl up and snore and not be bothered. Fox is more of an actress, who prefers center stage, usually a lap, which of course means kitty hair balls in the computer hard drive.

Although we had a dog when I was growing up, I became an instant convert when I got my first cat. She was a tabby named Tigre who was born on a closet floor in the house where I lived in college. In her youth, she was quite a good little traveler who loved riding in the car, perched on the back of my seat like a navigator. Then, when I moved to Florida, she became a real homebody with a fondness for warm sun and lizards. She moved in with my parents when I went to graduate school and developed a special kinship with them. From then on, she was their cat.

During my second semester in graduate school, a friend and I went to the humane society so she could buy a dog. She never found a dog, but I came away with a new cat. Demian, a one-eyed Himalayan, was named after the character in Herman Hesse's book and not after the devil in *The Omen*, as people always remarked when they heard the name. I had him fifteen years and thought of him as my I'm-going-to-be-published cat. He moved all over with me, from Tallahassee to Jacksonville to Boca Raton and Fort Lauderdale. Two years after my first book was published, he had to be put to sleep.

I was reading *Many Lives, Many Masters* at the time, a book on reincarnation written by a psychiatrist in Miami, and started wondering about reincarnation in the kitty kingdom. A couple of days later, I dreamed I went into the kitchen late one night for something to eat and Demian strolled in and began eating out of his bowl. I looked down at him and said, "You're dead." He replied that he wasn't. I got the feeling from this dream that it was okay for me to get another cat now. So on my fortieth birthday I got Fox. Although she has two eyes and doesn't look anything at all like Demian, they share many of the same characteristics and mannerisms.

Cats have definitely inspired my writing. In my series featuring husband and wife detectives Quin St. James and Mike McCleary, there are three cats. Merlin, the black cat and oldest, is most like Demian in personality. When I started a second series (Tango Key) under another name, I'd given my protagonist a cat. My editor suggested I use some other type of animal in that the McClearys already had three cats. So I gave her a skunk. But as the series progressed, I really missed having a cat in the scheme of things, so in the third book, a one-eyed cat named Unojo (One Eye) made an appearance.

The world is divided into cat people and dog people, and animals know it as well as we do. Look at the way stray cats find their way to homes inhabited by cat lovers, not dog lovers. They hide under cars owned by cat lovers. They camp on doorsteps owned by cat lovers.

I'm mush when it comes to my cat; Rob is far more practical. If Fox or Shelly refuse the evening's kitty cuisine, I open a can of people tuna, and do it even though I know that two days from now Rob is going to say, "Hey, where's that tuna I bought?" And there are Fox and Shelly, smiling ever so smugly.

T. J. MacGregor and Rob MacGregor are novelists who live in Florida. Rob's novels include six original Indiana Jones novels and one novelization, *Indiana Jones and the Last Crusade*. T.J. MacGregor has written twelve mysteries, including *Spree, Death Flats*, and *On Ice*. She also writes under the name Alison Drake; these novels include *Lagoon, Black Moon*, and *Tango Key*.

Axel Madsen

I've had Veruschka for fourteen years. She's a snotty ass of a cat. My agent, Jane Jordan Browne, conned us all into taking a kitten. We were visiting her house, and we were about to pick out another when they all ran behind the stove in the kitchen. Veruschka was a little slower than the others, being the runt of the litter, so we picked her. She's had a chip on her shoulder ever since. Of course, Veruschka runs my house, but she's smart enough not to let me know. She can outsmart me, but I can outsmart her, too. She eats sashimi at fourteen dollars a pound—not every day, but she has these tendencies. She travels with us an awful lot. She's very good on airplanes; she's commuted back and forth to California with us for years. She's definitely a Beverly Hills alley cat.

I've had other cats, but she's my favorite. I never grew up with animals, but they say when you don't have pets when young, you acquire them when you're older. We never had a dog because we travel too much. Veruschka is a sweet thing. She respects me and I respect her. We have an almost symbiotic relationship; after fourteen years, she knows where she is and what she can get away with and what she can't.

Of course, I have to let her in the room when I write. She likes to sleep on top of the monitor because it's warm. She hasn't yet mastered the art of hitting control-Z-delete, which would crash the computer and wipe out all of my text, but she tries this at least once or twice a day.

I wrote the biography of Andre Malraux because he had cats, and in the book I have several quotes about him and his cats. Chanel didn't have cats, but I wrote her biography anyway.

I rarely get an opportunity to elaborate on their catty lives in my writing. Because I concentrate on nonfiction, I can't make up stories about cats, so I don't think Veruschka's had an influence on my writing. If I wrote fiction—and I have—then I would write about cats, but I don't have the talent for it. I'm too much the journalist.

I find dogs to be a bore; they're real babies. You can't go away and leave a dog for a day. I appreciate cats' independence; you can never own them. They're aloof and they have their integrity. They are not whores like dogs, but then again, they will follow anyone who will feed them. There's a stand-backness about cats I find pleasant and kittenish and feline. Cats are very calming and soothing. Veruschka sleeps with us in the middle of the bed and pushes us around all night.

Writing is basically a solitary metier; it's between us and the white sheet of paper. We are solitary like cats.

Dog people can be as shameless as cat people; even more so. We don't even have shows like the dog people have. Look at how they march their dogs down runways. Of course, our pets wouldn't stand for it.

Axel Madsen is the author of many celebrity biographies, including *Chanel: A Woman of Her Own* and *Gloria and Joe: The Star-Crossed Love Affair Between Gloria Swanson and Joe Kennedy.* He is currently working on a biography of the actress Barbara Stanwyck. He lives in Pennsylvania.

99

Axel Madsen

Bobbie Ann Mason

I've had a lot of cats, and quite a number of them descended from the kittens born in 1973 to one lovely white stray named Ada. I still have Bilbo, one of her grandchildren, now seventeen and toothless. Bilbo's sister Bubbles—white, with one blue eye and one yellow—was the smartest cat I ever knew, and their sister

Alice, a small white cat with calico spots and tail, would not have been able to define *mouse*. But Alice was my sweetest cat, and she lived a long life despite her many troubles.

My favorite cat is Kiko. Kiko is the real-life model for the cat Moon Pie in *In Country*, the only character in the novel to have a real-life counterpart. Moon Pie, like Kiko, is black with a saucer face and white armpits. For the movie of *In Country*, Moon Pie was played by an orange-and-white cat, whose real name was Moon Pie. To fill the role, the animal trainer went to an animal shelter, rescued a cat, named him Moon Pie, and kept him for her own. I feel very proud that if my writing has accomplished nothing else, it saved this cat's life and gave him a good home. Moon Pie gave a wonderful performance in the movie. He got to lick tuna fish oil from Bruce Willis's chest, and he did some great meows.

Kiko is much like a moon pie, although his nickname is "The Fatburger." His mother was Himalayan, which accounts for the pie-face. He's very people-oriented and not much of an outdoorsman. He watched a mouse swimming in his water dish once, and on one memorable occasion he did catch a mouse in the kitchen and trotted nonchalantly through the living room with it, as if to say, "Oh, don't mind me, I'm only passing through with my mouse." It was interesting that he detoured through the living room so that I would be sure to notice the mouse.

Kiko sits on my desk in a round, sheepskin bed. He used to sit in an old manuscript box. He misses me when I go away, and he's usually eager to start our working day. He's my chief inspiration.

My funniest cat is Boone, a long-haired white cat with peach-blush points and blue eyes. He's funny because his feet are so huge and his winter ruff makes him look like a snow monkey. He also likes to drool when he sits in my lap purring, and his ruff gets soaked. By contrast, Albert, an orange tiger, is a serious cat who's usually outdoors, very busy on his rounds.

We had barn cats when I was growing up on a dairy farm, and I didn't develop an intimate relationship with a cat until I was grown and could have a house cat. All of our cats and dogs back then got killed on the road. My father was partial to white cats in his barn, and I have had nine white cats.

Cats are very hard to write about. My cats Blackie and Bubbles had small but important roles in a short story called "Offerings." And I put my mother's cat, Abraham, into my novel *Spence + Lila.* He seemed to belong in that landscape. A human doesn't have the authority to write fiction from a cat's point of view, and when animals are used as protagonists it's usually with human value, so it's not satisfying if you're after the experience of the animal.

Of course, the cats run the office and the household. They certainly are in charge of the dogs. They're great manipulators.

My current favorite literary cat is Hobbes in the comic strip "Calvin and Hobbes." Hobbes takes on a wisecracking, energetic, somewhat catlike personality. He's far wittier and more interesting than that greedy slob Garfield.

I don't think like a cat. They know so many things I don't know, and their perceptions are more acute. They know how to listen, and they're great motion detectors. Their basic approach is devious, because as stalkers they have to fool their prey. This is why they pretend so much, why they will never admit to their real motives, and why they seem to be so independent—they're really not. They are not confused by moral ambiguities, and they are free to make a trade with you—their sensuality and affection and comforting presence for yours (and your tuna fish supply).

Cats are not a substitute for anything. They are themselves. I usually prefer the company of cats to that of people, and if I ever have to go to the old-folks' home and they don't let me have cats, I reckon I won't last more than a week.

Bobbie Ann Mason is the author of *Love Life, Spence + Lila, In Country,* and *Shiloh and Other Stories.*

Sharyn McCrumb

I've always had Siamese up until now. When I just got out of college I had one named Amir, who was a beautiful seal point and very smart. He learned how to open doors. He was so heavy, and he would grasp the doorknob with his paws. His weight would turn the knob, and he would swing in and out of the room. He was fairly independent.

Then, after we got married, we got Simon. When he was a kitten, he was so tiny he used to sleep in a Kleenex box. After awhile I discovered that Simon is a very clichéd name for Siamese cats, but we'd never heard of it. In fact, we named him that because we had a Persian named Merlin, so we wanted to come up with another magician name. We got Simon Magus out of the Bible. But later, I met other people whose Simon was named after Paul Simon because they had another cat named Garfunkel. Then I met somebody else whose cat was named Simon after Simple Simon because he was stupid. They all came up with the name Simon for a Siamese cat and they all had their own reason for it.

Now, we have a cat named Sinead, who is one of Simon's descendants. The cat is named Sinead O'Connor, although the cat has more hair. We also have Pendragon, a black Persian, and Senga.

I think if you're going to be a writer, cats are the most compatible animals to have. They're quiet, they're not demanding, they're self-sufficient, and I think they're very intelligent. They don't take up a lot of psychic space like dogs do.

They hang out when I write, especially because the computer's warm. They like to sit on top of it, and also because I have all these books and papers spread out where I'm working. Of course, that is the ideal place to nap. They become sort of a floor display in my workspace.

My working hours are between eleven at night and three and four in the morning. That's the normal time for the cats to be awake, anyway, so we just put everyone else to bed and then go to work. Sometimes I'll go away and come back and my line ends with something like *and* and akjz appears, and you know somebody's walked across the sentence.

I prefer to have cats around rather than humans when I'm writing because they don't come up with ideas, they don't have little suggestions, and they don't try to interrupt me to tell me about their day. When I'm writing, cats make good companions because they believe in allowing each person to have the peace and quiet required: I won't bother you if you won't bother me. That's good for a writer, where a dog would say, "Let's go play ball! Let's go chase a squirrel! Let's go jogging!" You'll never have a cat saying, "Let's get out of here and get physical!"

They don't want to run the house, but they're always scheming to get out. We live close to a busy road, and I see them sizing up the family to decide who is the biggest patsy, thinking, "Which one of these people is stupid enough to let me slip out before they can get the door closed?" And the answer is usually small children; they'll pick the three-year-old as the pushover. About twice a day there's a mad dash to catch them before they get out.

Pendragon, because he's a city cat, doesn't have a realistic view of Mother Nature. We have a bird feeder that's way up off the ground. Pendragon would look up at the bird feeder at all the birds eating and he would meow and make that begging sound they make when I'm opening up a can. But he was directing it to the birds—like, "Would you please come down so I can catch you?" It didn't work.

Every now and then a mouse will get into the kitchen and Pendragon, the city cat, will get in a little practice, but of course the females are much better at mousing than he is. This goes all the way up to lions. The lionesses are the ones who do the hunting, not the big showy males. They're the businesswomen; he's just the show. He has this beautiful coat and just sits around and thinks he's Burt Reynolds, and she goes out and gets the job done.

Once we were having lunch and we had the door open because it was hot. Suddenly, the cat came bounding into the house and up on the table with a baby rabbit in his mouth. His whole attitude was, "Oh, lunch! May I join you?" Well, we were horrified and we took the bunny away from him, and it hadn't been hurt. So we put the cat in the house and turned the bunny loose and told it to go back to its mother. The cat gave us this look. He would look very pointedly at our lunch, then at us, and then at his empty plate, and the message was quite clear that he thought we were being incredibly selfish. So finally I had to go and open a can of cat food for him. I felt like I was paying a ransom.

Writing involves more thinking than actual writing. There are a lot of times when I'm writing that I don't want to be alone, but on the other hand, I can't be terribly interactive because I'm there but my mind isn't. With a cat, that's okay. He's perfectly willing to take a hand that's moving automatically while the brain is in Venice.

The Cat

on My

Shoulder

Sharyn McCrumb is an award-winning Southern novelist living in Shawsville, Virginia. She won an Edgar in 1988 for *Bimbos of the Death Sun,* and an Agatha for Best Short Story of 1990, "A Wee Doch & Doris." Her other novels include *If Ever I Return, Pretty Peggy-O, The Hangman's Beautiful Daughter,* and *Missing Susan.*

Barbara Mertz

At this moment, I have six cats. I've found that to be the maximum number. If it gets beyond that, they tend to squabble a lot. They don't really like each other much, but they get along all right. There are some spats now: somebody gets bored and swats someone else. I always seem to have one victim; it's that way with people, too. At the moment my tortoiseshell Dorothy is my victim. There's something about her! Everybody tries to beat her up. Nobody gets hurt seriously; I yell, "Knock it off, you guys," and break it up if I have to. I wish I could have a hundred, but that's not really practical.

I usually have a cat in each of my books. It's become a trademark, I guess. Once or twice I've substituted a dog, but I've gotten protests from dog people, who complain that I make them stupid and unattractive. I have two dogs, but I am definitely a cat person.

There seems to be an affinity between writers and cats, especially mystery writers and cats. I suppose it's their contemplative aspect. They're not as obtrusive as dogs. When they want your attention, they insist on having it, and then when they tire of it they walk away. It's more of an equal relationship with a cat; you don't feel as if you're the boss or the patron. I suspect people who tend to be loners prefer cats because they don't make excessive emotional demands.

I don't believe I think like a cat because I have no idea what cats are thinking. Sometimes I look at those furry faces and think, "What's going on in there, if anything?" It would make me very nervous to believe I thought like a cat.

I prefer the company of cats to that of most human beings. I find most humans boring, and I expect I bore them just as much. Cats are usually reasonable in their demands, with the exception of my huge Maine coon who, if he wants to rest peacefully on me at the computer, sits on my lap and stops any activity that's going on. He is probably the most dignified of all of my cats, but when he wants attention, he wants it *now* and he wants me to concentrate on him. He will allow me to read while I scratch him, but when he gets tired of it, he gets up and leaves. He doesn't demand more than he is due. I like that—mutual respect. And they're so beautiful, so fuzzy; I love the way cats feel.

I do find some cat people sickeningly maudlin. They dress their "kitties" up and tie bows around their necks, and talk about "baby pussy cats." The point is that cats are not people and they are not babies; they are a separate species with a dignity of their own, and I think it's degrading to treat them like children. I treat them like cats, and they treat me like, well, a rather large and stupid cat. Dog people are just as bad; they think dogs are superior. We *know* that cats are superior to dogs. I don't care what the intelligence tests tell me.

The popularity of Maine coon cats is a rather recent development.

I found out about them fifteen years ago from a friend who was one of the first breeders. I fell in love with them—the great big poofy things tromping around, all different shapes and sizes. I think anybody who sees one wants one. I have converted at least three of my friends after they've seen mine. Men particularly seem more attracted to them than to other cats because they're such big, macho-looking creatures. That's deceptive; they are really the gentlest of animals. My agent now has two Maine coon cats. They're great to sleep with; you don't need blankets or a hot water bottle. But they're very placid, and more dignified than other cats.

I'm not a big believer in ghosts despite the fact that I write mysteries for a living, but I could be convinced that there is some kind of mental communication between people and their pets. You can tell the difference between Out and Eat and Pet Me—at least I can. But I have actually had them convey a specific message. I had a Siamese, and we also had a hamster, who used to get out of his cage, to the fury of everybody, because he used to get in bed with people. You'd feel these cold little paws walking up and down your face. He got so cocky he drove the Siamese crazy. One evening she came downstairs, meowing in that strident voice Siamese have, and I broke off the conversation with my friend and said, "Damn, that hamster's out again!" I followed the cat up the stairs; she showed me where the hamster was, and I captured it and put it back in the cage. When I came back downstairs my friend was still gaping. She said, "How did you know what she said?" I said, "I don't know how I knew, but I knew immediately what she meant." Ever since then, I've wondered if there isn't some kind of mental rapport between animals and people.

Barbara Mertz is a mystery writer who lives near Frederick, Maryland. She has written twenty-five mystery-suspense novels under the name Barbara Michaels, and two dozen under her second pseudonym, Elizabeth Peters. Her latest books include *Vanish with the Rose*, by Barbara Michaels, and *The Snake, the Crocodile and the Dog*, by Elizabeth Peters.

David Morrell

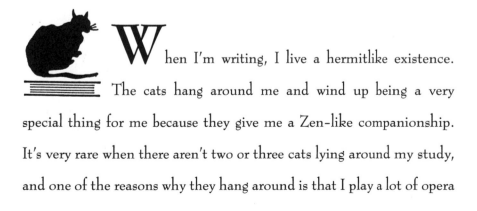

When I'm writing, I live a hermitlike existence. The cats hang around me and wind up being a very special thing for me because they give me a Zen-like companionship. It's very rare when there aren't two or three cats lying around my study, and one of the reasons why they hang around is that I play a lot of opera while I'm working. Today, for example, I listened to *Tosca* three times. I call them my opera cats because they seem to be absorbing some kind of charge from this music. I'm getting a pleasure from the music, but I'm also getting something from them. It's almost like they're storage batteries and I'm getting energy from them. They are purring away, generating the juice that keeps me going. They all gather as a clan and sleep in front of the speakers for eight hours. They especially like Puccini.

As long as I can remember, I've been surrounded by cats. My mother enjoyed cats. At one point we had twenty-eight cats in the house, which is more than I think is good for anybody. Two litters were born in my lap.

My favorite cat was a Siamese named Samantha, Sammy for short. I used Sammy in a book I wrote called *Testament,* a thriller involving paramilitary right-wing hate organizations. It begins with a cat so stupid it would walk over candles and set fire to itself, or sleep curled up on a television, roll over and fall off the back and get its claws hooked over the front. What you'd see is this little head and paws hanging over the top. I thought this was too unusual not to be used, so I put the scene with the cat in the first few pages because I wanted to do a fancy thing with hooking the reader. There's always one jerk in the neighborhood who hates cats, and this guy told me if he ever saw my cat outdoors he was going to kill it. He said he was going to put the cat in a burlap sack, tie it over the tailpipe of his car, and then start the car and asphyxiate it. At least I had to give him points for imagination.

What I did in the book was have our hero wake up in the morning and be downstairs with his family eating breakfast. He looks over and the cat's drinking milk out of a saucer. Suddenly, it falls into the milk and dies. He picks up the cat and thinks, it's that old guy down the street. He thinks the guy must have poisoned the cat in the night. He's thinking poison, poison, and he looks at the milk in the saucer, and he looks over at the kitchen table, and sees milk in the coffee, milk in the cereal, milk in the baby bottle, and he rushes and manages to stop everybody but the baby from drinking the milk, and the baby dies. That's on page three. To this day, I don't think this creep in my neighborhood knows I used him in the book.

There's something about the independence of a cat, and a cat is so elegant. My cats talk to me and tell me exactly what I need to know, whether they want to go out, or what they want to eat. I can tell from the different tones of their voices.

Anyone who has cats knows the cat runs the household. When the vet told me recently to give my cats only dry food, I told her that would be too difficult. She said to me, "You're the owner, that's the pet." But every morning at three a.m. I hear mrow, and if the tones tell me I want to go out, I want to be fed, or let's play, I respond. They definitely run the household; our schedule is dictated by them.

I think people who are attracted to dogs have different personalities than those who are attracted to cats. Dogs can be trained, but there's no way you're ever going to control a cat. People with cats are more existential and able to go with the flow. They're less concerned with controlling the circumstances. With my work, there's a real paradox because if I didn't control my work, I would never get anything done. But these cats represent a good balance that any good working writer must have.

The sense of discipline I must have in my writing is so strong it's easy to say, it's such a nice day, I'm going to take it off, and so I almost vicariously enjoy myself by watching these animals having a good time, and somehow it keeps me going. There is a very powerful spiritual connection.

My favorite literary cat has to be Bill the Cat from the comic strip Bloom County. I'm one of the proud owners of a Bill the Cat stuffed animal; it's sitting on top of my bookshelf. I think Bill's got to be right up there with T. S. Eliot's cats and Hobbes from the comic strip Calvin and Hobbes as far as literary cats go.

David Morrell is a novelist who lives in Iowa City. He is best known as the creator of the character Rambo in his 1972 novel *First Blood*.

Jan Morris

I've had cats all my life, and none of them has ever been ordinary. Our first pedigree cats were given to us by an American couple when we were living on a houseboat in Cairo. They gave us two small Siamese cats who would occasionally fall into the river and have to be whisked out, but lived quite happily on board. After that, I had a mixture of cats, until I came in contact with my first Abyssinian. Then I collected four of them, one right after the other. This lasted a large part of my life. A couple of years ago the last one died, and I began to fear it was too emotionally demanding to get another. They become such friends, and when you lose them it's like losing children or brothers and sisters. I thought maybe I shouldn't have another one, and I haven't since.

We don't have an Abyssinian now, but my partner Elizabeth has a Maine coon who's an extremely amiable cat and is named after the first Maine coon cat, Captain Jenks. I feel very attached to the fellow, but not the way I felt attached to Abyssinians. Maine coons are very fine animals. I like them very much.

I have written an awful lot about cats, but otherwise I think they have the same influence on me as on anyone who's working in their presence. Their very existence is soothing and serene and entertaining, and if you want a moment away from work, the cat is always prepared to do something with you—especially an Abyssinian. All you have to do is look at an Abyssinian and he's ready to play a game or have a conversation. They're a great diversion from work, as well as being soothing for it.

Having an Abyssinian is like having a great work of art. We live in the heart of rural Wales, so the Abyssinian is even more exotic here. Suddenly to come across one against our landscape, with the sheep and dogs, is a breathtaking experience.

Cats are not in charge of my household and never have been; that would be carrying things too far. I don't try to run their lives, and they're certainly not going to run mine. I'm definitely not going to be bossed around by a cat.

I like Kipling's *The Cat Who Walked by Himself* best, but I generally don't like cats in books because they're usually not my kind of cat. I like the Cheshire Cat in Alice because he's very strange.

It's a rather impertinent thing to say, but I do believe I think like a cat. I feel very much at home in the mental presence of a cat. I find myself behaving rather catlike, and I've picked up some of their habits. I narrow my eyes with affection toward them. I admire and envy them, and I'd like to be more like a cat. I like their ease. They define ease in every way. They can take things pretty much in stride. Because they're so supple, they can fall into any posture they like. They can jump and move very lightly, and they can take over a house if they want to. Their entire approach to life seems easy, as if they have no real problems to cope with.

I tend to find cats more than they find me. I don't know if it's true, but I think cats tend to go more toward people who don't like them. But I think maybe I overdo it a bit; they see me coming along and they run away.

Everything I've described about cats is what writers would like them to be: unobtrusive, kind, and available when you want them. They don't make a fuss yapping and licking you, and if you're writing, they keep quiet. I think for the writer they're almost the ideal companion. But there are also writers who are just as keen about dogs as I am about cats.

I think Americans tend more than Europeans to be shameless about their cats. The cat is more of a cult figure in America than over here.

I'm constantly struck by that look in the eye of a cat—especially Abyssinians. You know the look, where they get you in a gimlet stare and they see their eyes in your eye. I'm sure the look has a meaning, but I've never been able to find out what it is. It comes out of nowhere, a kind of smouldering look. I don't know if it expresses resentment; maybe it's a resentment at being domesticated at all. I think somewhere in the depths of their subconscious they regret it. Wouldn't you?

Jan Morris has published some twenty-five books of history, travel, fiction, and autobiography.

Marcia Muller

I never had a cat until I was in my mid-twenties, and since then there's been a steady progression of them through my household. My cats frequently end up as characters in my novels. I write a series about a private investigator named Sharon McCone; her first cat was actually my cat, Watney. He was an unusually oversized creature. When I'd take him to the vet, they'd ask, "My God, what *is* it?" Eventually I had to kill the fictional Watney off—nothing graphic, just to illustrate a point about change in life. Right after that, I got hold of my present cats, Ralph and Alice, and introduced them into the series.

When I write, Ralph sometimes sleeps on top of my file cabinet. There's a big oak tree right outside my office window; both cats have discovered that it's the best way to enter the house. They don't believe in doors. They climb the tree, drop down on the roof, and then bang on the window to be let in. Sometimes I feel like I'm their door—or window—man.

They're in total charge here, and they know it. We spend a great deal of our time as servants to the cats. I'm constantly opening little cans of food. One has a special diet and loves the stuff he's not supposed to eat; the other's taken to only eating in the pantry. It's quite ridiculous to put up with this sort of thing, but I guess I'm just a soft touch where cats are concerned.

Ralph and Alice are mindreaders. When one of us is going to be traveling, they can tell beforehand, even before the dreaded suitcases come out. I think they can read a certain level of tension in us before a trip as we're rushing around to get things done. They get very quiet and suspicious and hostile, and when the suitcases appear, they panic. We travel a fair amount, and I would never take them with us—they're yowlers. Actually, they're quite content being left in their own home, because, after all, it's only the servants going away—not anyone really important.

Do cats actually think? I'm not sure what they do. There's a great cartoon by B. Kliban showing a cat sitting in a corner with one of those thought bubbles over its head, and what it's thinking is an image of the corner. I think that's about the extent of it; cats are pretty literal minded.

Cats do serve as child substitutes for some people. They talk about their cats and carry their pictures around. But of course *I'm* not like that . . . although I do have pictures I will show to anyone who wants to see them. I suppose that, to some extent, all pets are child substitutes; some people carry it to extremes, if they've never had children, or their children have grown up and they miss them.

Two cats is my absolute max. I've had as many as four at one time, and it was just unmanageable. But they always find me—strays, the neighbors' cats. I turn them away because Ralph and Alice are quite enough. They pretend to hate each other, but when we're not at home they're best buddies and keep each other entertained.

Why do I like cats? They're capable of being very loyal and forming what passes for an emotional attachment without giving in totally and losing anything of themselves. It's a trait I admire in humans—something we might all strive for.

Marcia Muller has authored or coauthored nineteen mystery novels, eleven of which feature San Francisco private investigator Sharon McCone. In addition, she has co-edited ten anthologies of short stories and a critical work on mystery and detective fiction. Her 1989 novel, *The Shape of Dread*, received the American Mystery Award for the best private eye novel, and she received a Private Eye Writers of American Shamus award for best short story of 1990. The next novel in the McCone series, *Pennies on a Dead Woman's Eyes*, was published by the Mysterious Press in July of 1992.

Joyce Carol Oates

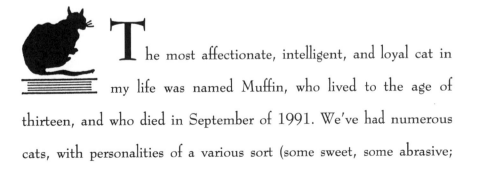 The most affectionate, intelligent, and loyal cat in my life was named Muffin, who lived to the age of thirteen, and who died in September of 1991. We've had numerous cats, with personalities of a various sort (some sweet, some abrasive;

most quite winning, but one or two frankly disagreeable), but thus far, Muffin remains the most extraordinary, and the most beloved.

Cats and kittens were always a part of our life, since earliest childhood in Millersport, New York, on my family's farm. Cats do seem to be drawn to me, perhaps sensing a kindred spirit. Since I don't believe that cats "think" as we do, I seriously doubt that I think "like a cat."

Alice Adams asks the question, "What does it mean to love an animal?" A profound question, not easily answered. I think one can only *experience* it.

My labyrinthine novel *Bellefleur* has a cast of several highly individualized cats, including the exotic Persian, Mahalaleel. My short story "The Seasons" is a fictionalized account of Muffin and his brother Tristram, who were foundlings. Another story, "The White Cat," is a Gothic transfiguration of a cat of ours named Miranda, who died some years ago but was reborn as a malevolent presence in this story to be included in *The Sophisticated Cat,* an anthology of prose and poetry edited by Daniel Halpern and me for NAL/Dutton in 1992.

I don't know if Lewis Carroll's Cheshire Cat is my favorite literary cat but he is my oldest acquaintance among such cats, and remains exemplary in a mysterious way.

I'm extremely fond of cats—obviously!—for their beauty, their discriminatory passions, their much-lauded independence, and their capacity for devotion. Like all animals, they remain enigmas: "domesticated," while still, at heart, *Felis sylvestris,* the wild cat of primitive times.

Joyce Carol Oates is the Roger S. Berlind Distinguished Professor in the Humanities at Princeton University and the author of twenty novels, eleven collections of short stories, and many other literary works.

Jay Parini

I believe there's a place in the world for moderately devoted fans of cats, like me. I'm not a fanatic about them. If I were a fanatic, I'd probably let them live indoors. The indoor cat is a bastardized version of the wild animal. I have barn cats instead. I've always felt that animals were meant to live outdoors; there's something corrupt about letting them live indoors. I think cats deserve to live outdoors because they really are miniature versions of lions and tigers.

What all pets represent is the self of the owner: projections of the owner that are reified, given fur, and allowed to move around. When you go to a shrink today, they say talk about the little boy inside you. In some ways, I suspect that shrinks would get a lot farther if they'd ask their clients to talk about the little animal inside them. I think I have several cats inside me. They're independent, and they go away for three weeks and come back again happily, no questions asked. They can live in the forest and forage for mice and moles; they like to dive under hay piles in the barn.

Cat loyalty is much more ironic than dog loyalty. The only type of loyalty we can have in the postmodern age is ironic loyalty, and I love that. Dogs are so damn un-ironic; the expressionless face of a dog is so horrific. Cat faces just naturally pucker up into a wry smile, and I love that about them.

Last summer, we had three mother cats, all of whom had litters, for a total of twenty-three cats. The barn is connected to the house, so, with twenty-three cats, our rule about no cats in the house began to fail somewhat, but, generally speaking, they lived outdoors. The babies all got some type of eye infection, so it was quite a ritual putting eyedrops in the eyes of twenty-three cats; that's forty-six eyes being dripped into three times a day. The entire summer was devoted to dripping drops into cats' eyes. I think of that as the summer of the cats.

At the end of the summer, there was a town fair in Middlebury, a peasant market that our church holds. My wife and I decided we had to get rid of these cats, keeping only the original three. So, we took all the babies, their eyes all nice and fixed, and put them in boxes and sat our kids down with them. The sign above the box said Free Cats, but in the first day or two, hardly any were given away. Then I realized suddenly that we live in a capitalist culture and nobody really believes that you can get something for nothing. So the next day I put up a sign that said Baby Cats, $2 Each, and they sold right away.

Cats have crept in and out of my poems and my novels, but they're very much like my barn cats—they come in out of the wilderness, camp out in a paragraph or two, and then disappear.

I do think of writers and cats as being especially amicable. A cat is a kind of symbol of the imagination in a weird way. And like all flights of imagination, they come and go. They inhabit you for a brief period, and then they go away.

Cats have always hovered over my writing, but not in a physical sense. I like to sit at my desk and look out and see my cats playing in a field near my house. I love to see them perilously leaping from limb to limb on an old crooked cedar rail fence, watching how they balance, how they fall and catch themselves. Their gracefulness and ease strikes me as the ideal form of the English sentence. The way each claw should connect to the next claw in its own quiet way, jumping from limb to limb, and the way cats glide and move through the air and the way they right themselves is ultimately the way a paragraph or a poem should finally come to rest on its feet and stand elaborately erect and well-balanced. After I finish watching my cats outside and return to my poetry or prose, I feel I have a kind of supple grace that was inspired by that physical movement. There's an easy transference for me from the exterior world of the cat to the interior world of the text.

Cats have such perfect posture, and that's the most marvelous thing about them; they stretch, and that's the way to live in the world. People don't stretch enough, and that's why they're so cramped. We can learn a lot from cats.

Jay Parini, a poet and novelist, teaches at Middlebury College in Vermont. His recent books include *Town Life*, a book of poetry, *The Last Station*, a novel, and most recently the novel *Bay of Arrows*.

Barbara Paul

My favorite cat was an alley cat named Schroeder, who lived a long life and died six years ago. The two cats I have now are a couple of white cats named Godfrey and Daniel. Remember W. C. Fields and what he said, back when you couldn't say "goddamn" in the movies? He said *"Godfrey Daniel."* Godfrey and

Daniel had lived around the corner from me and had been abandoned. They figured I was the biggest patsy in the neighborhood, and so about four years ago they moved in on me. I had been catless for a while, and thought I would never have another one, because I had to have my last one put to sleep—which I swore I would never do, but I had never watched a cat starving to death. He'd grown so old his body was no longer manufacturing the enzymes he needed to digest food.

I've always had cats around. When I work, one of them sleeps in a plastic crate under the computer while the other one's all over the place. He gets on the top of my hightop leather chair and kibbitzes. Sometimes they'll knock things over intentionally to get my attention. They'll jump up on the worktable and keep pushing little things off until I decide to give them some attention. Maybe it's just a paper clip or a pen, something like that, but they do seem to know what's breakable and what isn't. One of the cats presses on the computer keyboard when he sees me doing it, but I don't allow them up on the table with the computer because hair can get in it. In fact, that's the one thing I don't like about cats, all that hair. Sometimes it's like living with Vincent from the TV series *Beauty and the Beast*.

I once wrote a cat named Godfrey Daniel into a mystery, *But He Was Already Dead When I Got There*. I also had a story in the anthology *Cat Crimes*, with a cat in it that was partially based on one of the cats I have now.

My cats are pretty demanding as far as food is concerned. Armageddon would have to be delayed if they were hungry, but other than that they are pretty well behaved. Daniel eats everything; Godfrey is more fussy. They both hate sardines. I once opened a can for them and they gave me this look that said, "You've got to be kidding," and walked away. I haven't tested them on caviar yet. Once, I did feed them baby food when one of them had an upset stomach.

Dogs are heavy and put their feet all over you. Cats just purr. It's soothing to have a cat around. I like cats because I think they're funny; they give me one good laugh every day. For instance, Godfrey sometimes gets caught half in a drawer and half out, scrabbling around the air with his hind legs, trying to get out. Godfrey just now jumped up on the back of the chair, wondering what this phone conversation is about. He seems to blame me for bad weather. Every time it rains or snows he comes in and roars at me. I honestly believe he thinks I can turn off the bad weather the way I turn off a light. And Daniel turns on the television when it gets too quiet for him.

I like the way they feel curled up against me. They don't talk back, lie, or nag—well, they do nag a little sometimes. But when I feel like orating, they make a perfect audience. Except when I sing. I can't sing when Daniel's around. When I do, he comes up to me and meows and butts me with his head and starts patting me with his paws; he's trying to comfort me. He thinks I'm in pain. I know I'm no singer, but I'm not *that* bad.

Barbara Paul is a former academic who quit teaching at the University of Pittsburgh to write full-time. She's written both science fiction and mysteries. Her most recent book is *You Have the Right to Remain Silent*, and her next book is *The Apostrophe Thief*.

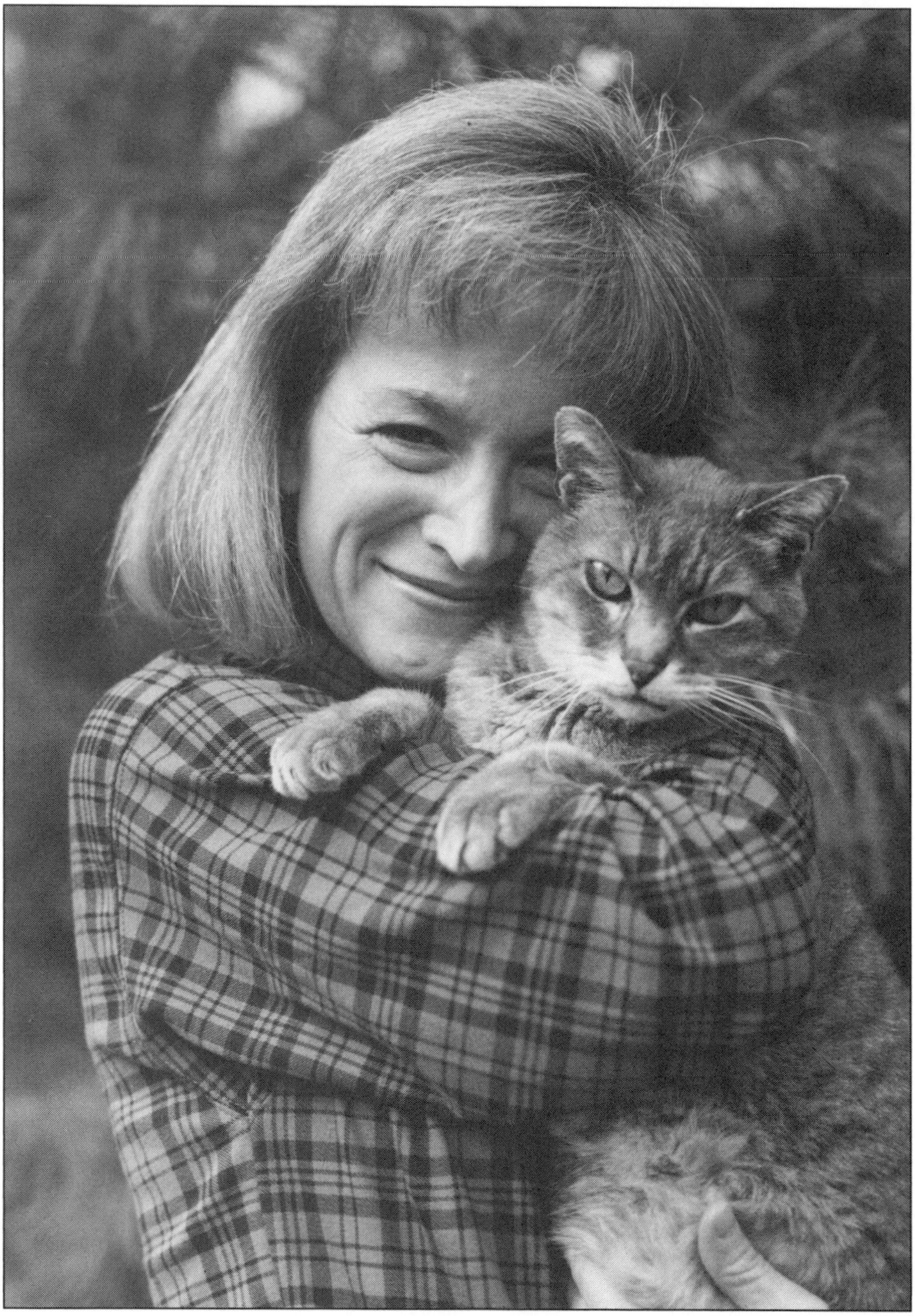

Nancy Pickard

The first cat I had was a cat named Buttons, a big yellow cat, who was roundly disliked by everybody in the family but me. She had an awful personality, but her main claim to fame was that she had a litter of one kitten, and she had that kitten on a rocking chair during an episode of "Peter Gunn," when I was in high school. We named it Bows, so then we had Buttons and Bows.

Now I have Andrew, a cat I've had for almost nineteen years. He is an enormous gray cat. I think he's terribly handsome, and he just appeared at my door one day in the hands of two little boys who had found him. I took him in and it was clear from the beginning that this cat knew exactly who he was and who he wanted to be, and where he wanted to go, and all I had to do is just stand back and let him be. And so I did, and we've gotten along beautifully. He has never been intimidated by dogs. I used to have an American Eskimo dog, who's a very hyper kind of dog. He used to race around the dinner table and the cat would stand on top of the table and then jump on the dog's back, and then off they'd go through the house.

Andrew developed diabetes a couple of years ago, and I have to give him insulin shots every evening. It's gotten to where he lets me know when it's time for his shot. Not only does he not give me any problems, but if I'm late he comes in and tells me, so I figure he must know what's good for him.

He taught himself to go to the bathroom in the toilet, but he's never learned to flush. It's a little embarrassing when people come to call and there are paw prints on the toilet seat.

Andrew used to be quite a hunter. It used to look like all the animals from Noah's Ark had ended up dead on my front doorstep. It wasn't one of his more endearing qualities, but he's gotten a bit old for that.

I'm convinced Andy can talk; he can say milk and out. Andrew is just this incredible calm Buddha of a cat. He's into the zen of being a cat, and so he was never a bully, he was just never intimidated. He doesn't run the household; he's much more discreet than that. He's worked himself into the household so that as long as he's fed and gets to drink his milk, and go out when he wants to, he's fine. He doesn't have to demand anything; you know, when you're Buddha, you just exist.

For a long time, Andy would sit on my lap or curl up in my out basket while I wrote, but he's so big—he weighs eighteen pounds—that it's hard to type over him, so I don't encourage him to sit on my lap anymore. He still hangs out in my office, but I don't let him sit on my lap. The reason is that frequently he wants to nudge my chin, asking me to pet him, and I can't do everything at one time. I'm planning to put a cat in my next mystery, and I think this cat will end up being modeled somewhat on Andy.

When I was pregnant, I was sick for awhile and had to stay in bed. My husband accidentally ran over the cat, who received a broken pelvis as a result. The vet told us to put him in a playpen with a litter box and food and water. I was down at the end of a long hall where I was sick, and one day that cat climbed out of the playpen and dragged himself down the hall into the bedroom where I was, and he stood there and looked up at me. I thought, this cat wants to be here with me, and if he went to all this trouble to get here, he's going to stay here. So he spent the rest of his convalescence on the bed with me.

Cats are supposed to be mysterious. There's something about cats being able to slip in and out—like my cat, who tends to slip in and out of houses in the neighborhood. God only knows what sorts of scenes he witnesses. Cats are also apparently loners, which I don't agree with, because my cats have always been very social creatures. Not particularly with strangers, but here at home Andy always wants to be where the people are.

Cat people are without sympathy for people who don't like cats, and they can be shameless in their disregard for other people's feelings. I have no patience with people who don't like cats, and I've been known to judge people on how they get along with my animals. I think one of the reasons I married my husband is that when he first came over he went straight past me to say hello to my cat and dog. I thought, this man's all right.

I like the sensuous quality of cats. I can almost feel what it feels like to them to stretch that long back, work those shoulders, bring those hips up, and stretch those legs. I love the way they feel; I love to stroke them.

Nancy Pickard is a mystery writer who lives in Kansas. She is the author of seven mystery novels in the Jenny Cain series, including *Say No to Murder*, *Dead Crazy*, and *Bum Steer*. She is a former president and founding member of Sisters in Crime, the national association of women mystery writers, and has won the Anthony, Macavity, and Agatha awards for her novels.

Marge Piercy

All of my books of poetry, beginning with *The Moon Is Always Female,* have occasional poems about my cats in them. Arofa, a very intelligent Siamese, and Cho-Cho, a beautiful but ditzy Maine coon cat, were the first cats of mine who figured in my poetry. All of the cats I now have appear in poems in the last decade. My husband Ira Wood and I have four: brother and sister sable Burmese Jim Beam and Colette, and two Korats, Dinah and Oboe, mother and son. I recently wrote a poem about a cat I had when I was aged twelve to fifteen, a gentle tabby named Fluffy, who was poisoned by the boy next door when my parents sold their house to a black family.

At readings, people will sometimes come up to me and ask me how my cats are by name. On the other hand, I have met cats named for me. It's disconcerting (Now Marge Piercy, if you don't use your litter box, I'm going to pour water on your tail. Oh, that Marge Piercy, there she is in heat again!), but I don't really mind it.

My husband thinks I'm a cat fetishist, but I'm really not. I confine myself to mugs with cats on them and occasional cat cards to other cat people I know. Both my husband and I have modeled cats in our novels after cats we've had. In my novel *Fly Away Home,* the cats bear a strong resemblance to Jim Beam and Colette. The cats in Ira Wood's novel *Going Public* are based on Dinah and Oboe.

As novelists, I think what intrigues us the most about cats is how much human behavior they prove to be mammalian behavior, and yet they are totally other. When Jim Beam is frustrated in his desire to go out, he will turn and hit his sister for no good reason. When Colette misses a leap, she will pretend she meant to examine some interesting invisible object on the floor. Each individual cat's status in the group is volatile—but Dinah, who weighs half of what the others weigh, is almost always top cat because she is the most passionate in her willfulness and will back down only sometimes to her son. Colette, who is a big cat, has the self-image of the runt of the litter that she was; Dinah, the size of a kitten, has the self-image of a lioness and behaves accordingly.

I don't consider any of my cats psychic, although Oboe has a sense of smell and of hearing that would confound anyone studying normal sensory apparatuses. He can be asleep on my bed (where, incidentally, he was born). A can of tuna fish (they get tuna once a week as a treat—dolphin-safe tuna) is opened one floor down at the other end of the house. He does not do this for any other food. He will be in the kitchen under the can opener in twenty seconds flat. On the other hand, when I am calling him to take his pill (he has asthma), he is deaf until the moment I go to grab him. Then he vanishes. He is the only one of my cats who is overweight, but he can fit into an envelope and hide in my desk when it is time to avoid a pill.

I did have one cat who was empathic, Arofa. I could communicate with her by touching her and communicating strong emotion about something. She not only did not kill birds, she ratted on Cho-Cho and various other strays I had taken in when they did so. You could really communicate with her, and she was very good at communicating back. When I moved from New York to Cape Cod, I had to go away for a month to do a residency to pay the plumber and the electrician. When I came back, she took me around the property and showed me all of the wonderful places she had discovered. She was a cat who fixed on a couple of people only. She used to bite my lovers. She resented them. She was fiercely possessive and jealous.

Basically I find cats good company. The cats I have now are pretty accepting of friends and guests. They hang out with one another a great deal, but each one of them wants some time from each of us, and they like to be talked to. Each one has worked out a personal niche in the day that is that cat's particular property—when we drink coffee in bed in the morning, when we take our baths, when we write, when we listen to music or watch TV, even when we do exercises. What strikes me is how individual they are, brother and sister, mother and son, each totally unlike the others, but all affectionate with one another and with us. The notion that cats are not social is not borne out by the behavior of mine.

Marge Piercy is the author of twelve collections of poetry, including *The Moon Is Always Female.* She has written eleven novels, all still in print, including *Woman on the Edge of Time, Vida, Braided Lives, Gone to Soldiers,* and *Summer People.* Knopf published her latest novel, *He, She and It,* last winter. She is also the poetry editor of *Tikkun.* Her fiction and poetry have been translated into fourteen languages. She is married to the writer Ira Wood and lives in Wellfleet on Cape Cod.

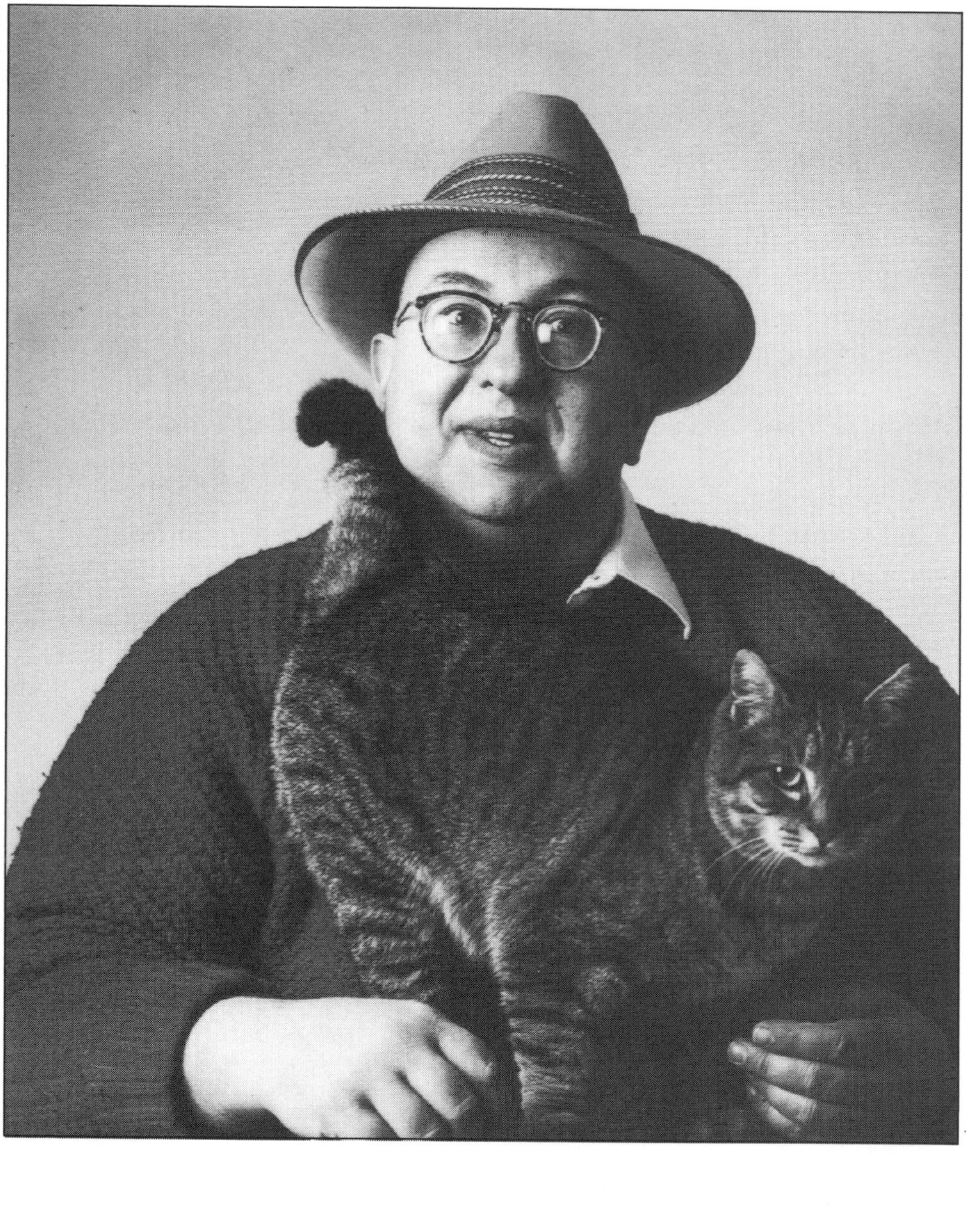

Daniel Pinkwater

There have been cats around here for years. I've outlived a number of cats by now, and then there are some I haven't. We have a nice assortment of cats, and I superstitiously never count them. There may be seven, there may be nine.

There's Charles, a Manx cat who came from the local shelter.

When we first moved to the country eleven years ago, we thought we needed a barn cat. We're city people, and the idea of keeping a cat out in the barn seemed a little cruel, but we needed something to keep the vermin down. We went to the shelter and said we needed a barn cat. They brought out a long-haired Manx cat, tailless, with a rag doll quality. They called him Big Mouth because he was very noisy. They had hidden him week after week from the sadistic old vet, who came every week and euthanized everything in sight. He had no private clients because everyone knew he murdered animals. They would put Big Mouth in the closet and turn up the radio so the vet wouldn't find him. We took him home and put him in the barn, where he immediately began to complain. He was indifferent to mousing; he would catch maybe one mole a year just to keep up his union membership. He would beat on the windows and howl at us. I interpreted it as, "Bosses! sitting inside drinking coffee! Here I am in the barn with nobody for company but mice!" Charles took ill. The vet diagnosed him as having something that would be fatal soon, so we took him in to keep him warm and comfort him in his last days. Of course it was a misdiagnosis; that was eight years ago, and he's been inside ever since.

My wife has a quality such that animals wild and domestic fall in love with her—including me. It got so that the barn rats would jump up and down squeaking their happiness whenever she went out there. She would shout at them and stamp her feet and say, "I don't want you, go away," and they would squeak, "Jill, Jill, Jill," which is cute in a cartoon but disgusting in person. So, finally we had to thin them out. I hid in a horse stall with my high-powered air riffle. There wasn't a rat in sight. When Jill came in, five or six rats came out waving their little paws at her. And then I was to pop one off. They don't just drop dead when you shoot them, they take off preferably to die in the wall where they'll stink and haunt you. So, I shot one, and it gave her a dirty look just before it died, like, "How could you do this to me?" It ran out of the barn door right into the mouth of Charles, who, at the time, was ambling around the corner. He thought he'd killed it. He laid it out by the kitchen door and posed next to it until sundown, waiting for somebody to come by and take a photo. He was very proud.

For a long time, Charles was my office cat. I sat in an office chair, a typist's chair. If the typist—in this case, me—leans forward for a cup of coffee or to sharpen a pencil, Charles neatly jumps in between my back and the backrest, and stays there. I lean back and try to crush him. He likes it. Of course I wouldn't really crush him, but as much crushing as I'm willing to do, Charles likes. If I remove him, the next time there's two inches of air between me and the chair, he's there. After a while, I quit removing him and work in a tilted-forward posture for several hours. I've developed a slight back condition I blame on him.

I didn't expel him from my office for that, but I did for throwing up in my computer printer repeatedly. I don't think it was any comment on what was coming out of it, but it's dangerous for him and me, so I banished him. He's an accommodating fellow; right now, he's between my wife's back and her chair.

Writers need to have a small engine humming in the room with them; it's very comforting. I liked to write with a cat by my side until I got an electric typewriter and, later, a computer, because that little purring and breathing created a nice sort of atmosphere. Of course, the electric typewriter hummed in the same way, so I told the cat to take a hike—into the next room.

Cats tend to be very insistent about getting their way, which can lead to fights. A cat wants to be on the table; you don't want it to be on the table. This can go on all day. They'll usually wear you down. It's humiliating to be defeated by an animal whose brain is the size of a walnut.

Daniel Pinkwater is a writer of books for children and young adults, and has written two collections of essays: *Fishwhistle* and *Chicago Days, Hoboken Nights*. He is a commentator for National Public Radio and is currently working on a novel. He lives in upstate New York.

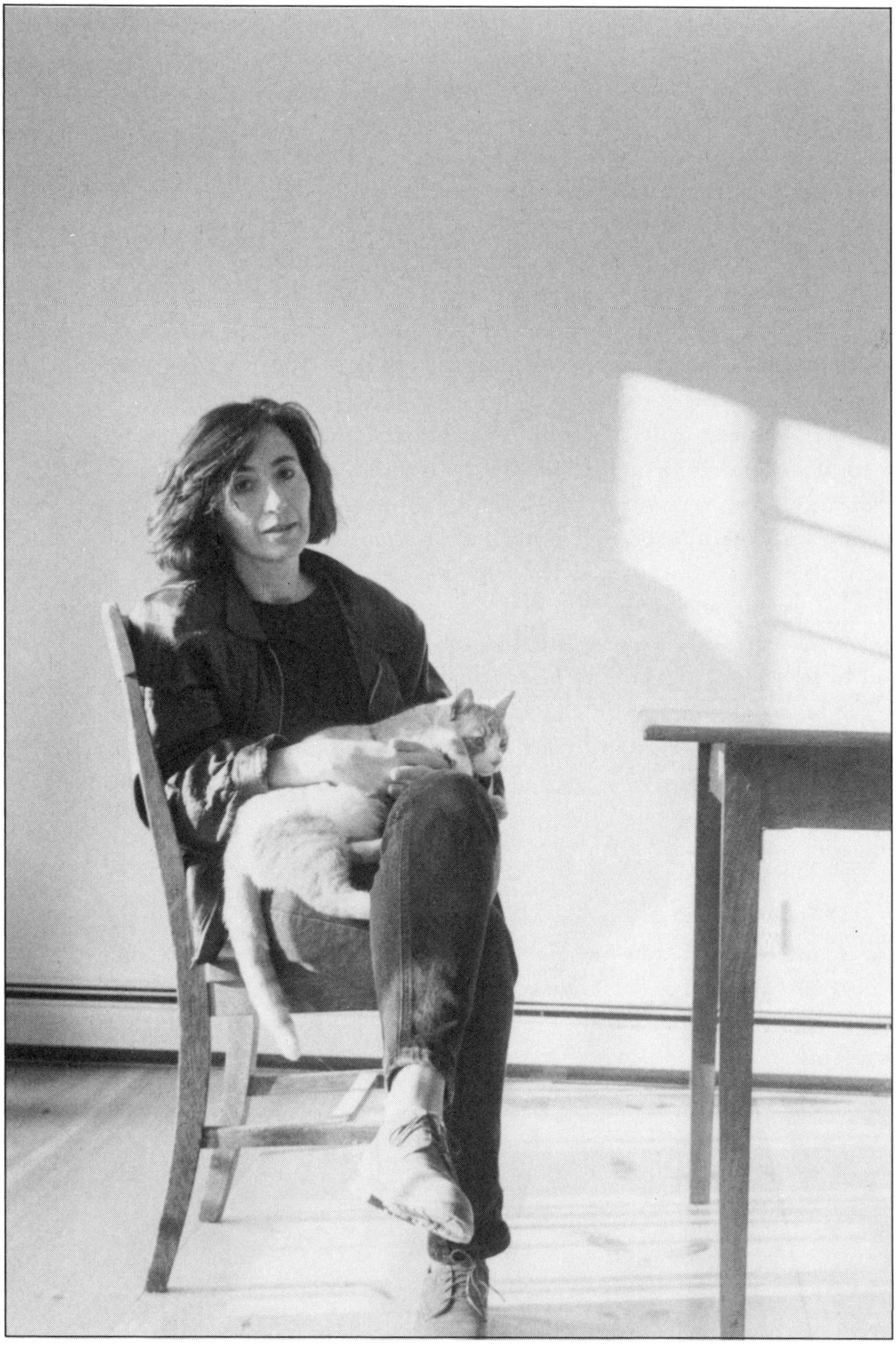

© JUDY LINN

Francine Prose

I've only had two cats in my life. The first one was a wild cat that adopted us, but it was a crazy barn cat and wouldn't come in the house. The cat we have now is my first real cat; it's named Geronimo. The cat got its name because when the kids were little they used to pick it up and throw it and yell Geronimo.

The cat is actually closer to my kids than to me or my husband, and sleeps with my younger son. One thing I'm proud of is that Geronimo has never used the litter box. We live in the country, so the cat just goes outside. He usually has to go out at three in the morning, so he runs the household in the sense that he makes my husband get up and let him out; otherwise, he's just a member of the family.

I've written about this cat in some stories, but I've noticed that I'm much more directly autobiographical about my cat than I am about myself or anybody else. We acquired Geronimo when a friend in the neighborhood called us up one morning and said there was something he wanted us to see behind his house. We went over and saw a huge, illegal medical waste dump. He took us back to his house and showed us a kitten in terrible shape who had been wandering around. He said the cat needed a home. He already had a cat, so he didn't want to take it. There was something about seeing the dump that made it impossible for us not to take the kitten. This was five years ago, and we've had Geronimo ever since.

I've put him in stories, and I have one story that's very much about him called "Amateur Voodoo." It came out in *Boulevard Magazine*. He doesn't hang around when I write, however, because he tends to hang out underneath my desk and play with the computer cables, and that's kind of distracting. Cats are low-maintenance compared to dogs. A cat can be there without being there; that is, be in a room but not up in your face. Writers tend to be very distracted, so I think they're better with low-maintenance pets, but then again, they have children, which are extremely high-maintenance.

In some ways, I would like to think like a cat, but I believe I think in a more complicated way than my cat, as intelligent as my cat is. What I like about cats is their great dignity, and I would like to imagine I have something of that. I don't like the fact that some of my closest friends are allergic to them. There are certain cats I find less aesthetic than others. I mean, extremely vocal cats get on my nerves. I also have some friends who have hairless cats, the Rex cats, and although I'm sure if they were my cats I'd grow to love them, I find them difficult to cozy up to. They have a ratlike appearance, but maybe if they were my cats I'd feel very differently.

Cats don't usually follow me around, but they do follow my husband around; it's kind of eerie. We'll go to someone's house or a party and soon all of the cats in the house will be sitting on top of him. Who knows if this is psychic or not, but my younger son's school bus comes home at four o'clock every day, and the cat is sitting there at the end of the driveway waiting for him. I'll forget, but the cat will remember. He doesn't do that on Saturday and Sunday.

There's something very doglike about our cat. He follows us when we go on walks; he has that doglike loyalty you don't usually associate with cats.

Once we had a misunderstanding with our neighbor. The cat had been going over to eat at the neighbor's for months, and somehow our neighbor had gotten the impression that Geronimo was a stray cat, so this neighbor took him down the road and let him out. My husband and son went to look for the cat. Fortunately, this cat has a great personality. They found it was eating its way down the road, which meant it went down the road eating dinner at a different house every night. We were able to trace its progress. It ended up at a house of some friends of ours who recognized it and brought the cat back.

Francine Prose is a novelist and short-story writer who lives in upstate New York. Her books include *Bigfoot Dreams, Hungry Hearts,* and *Women and Children First: And Other Stories.*

Cokie Roberts

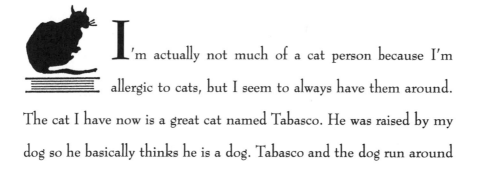I'm actually not much of a cat person because I'm allergic to cats, but I seem to always have them around. The cat I have now is a great cat named Tabasco. He was raised by my dog so he basically thinks he is a dog. Tabasco and the dog run around

together and do very boisterous kinds of things. As a result, he is extremely playful, and more like a puppy than a cat.

Tabasco is an orange marmalade cat. I like Tabasco sauce and always carry it in my purse, so my daughter, who got me the cat, decided he looked like the color of Tabasco. He's a spicy little cat, and since I like Tabasco, she decided to give me this Tabasco cat.

His predecessor was a black cat named Night Night. Obviously, he had been named by small children. He was a lovely sedate old cat. He hated the dog, but when this kitten came into the house, they became best friends.

Tabasco is not my boss; he's just an adorable little cat who seems to be a perpetual kitten. He must be a hunter cat in nature because he loves to dip his paw into water looking for fish. He also likes to open kitchen-cabinet doors to get to the food I put up high to keep it away from the dog. Tabasco also sits on the newspaper when I'm trying to read it, sits on my desk when I'm trying to work, and sits on my computer when I'm trying to write. In this way, he runs the house, but he's basically just a funny, cute cat.

For years we lived in Greece, which is completely overrun by cats. And people over there don't have cats as pets; the cats are strays who wander around the tavernas. It was always said that you'd know how good a taverna was by how many cats were there. Cats would always find us and follow us around, but we were a likely group because we had small children at the time, who were nothing but indulgent to these cats.

Cats are much cleverer and devious than I; I'm much more straightforward. I'm doglike in that way. I like cats when they aren't quite so haughty, and I also like all of the normal things about cats, such as when they come up and rub against me, or sit on my lap with their motor running—all of those things. Since I'm allergic to them, my eyes swell, but I still put up with them like an idiot. I live on Primatene at night because Tabasco sleeps with me, the little creep.

I don't attribute all of these great qualities to cats like other people do, such as being psychic. I've had much more psychic experiences with dogs. I've met many dogs who know when I'm leaving, and who disappear when they decide it's time somebody's going to die. I've dealt with dogs who deal with death in an extremely psychic way.

My last cat would only eat cat food. The cats we had in Greece would eat anything. Tabasco is very fond of any kind of food, and he'll take flying leaps onto the stove while I'm cooking. It scares me to death that he's going to burn himself, but so far he's managed to avoid it. He'll eat anything I'm working on, and when I'm cooking it he'll put his face in it. It's not pleasant. What's worse is when I'm eating breakfast; he put his face in my cereal bowl. I throw him off the table, but it doesn't do any good.

The other night I had my twin two-year-old nieces staying with me, and both the cat and dog got so jealous they got into a flying routine where they chased each other around and jumped all over the place so that I would pay attention to them instead of the babies. It was clearly a conspiracy. They have a lot of conspiracies. The cat pushes things off high shelves so that the dog can get them. They work as a team.

Sometimes I prefer their company to humans, but that goes without saying in that I cover politics.

Russell Baker once wrote a column about the fact that presidents who had daughters and dogs were used to faithful, loving creatures who would love them no matter what, which created a certain arrogance in Johnson and Nixon. Whereas if you were a president with sons and cats, you discovered what it was like to raise creatures that would have nothing to do with you, and who would treat you like a piece of dirt, which was the case with Ford, who was a much more humble politician. This theory also applied to presidents who had sons and cats and daughters and dogs, but at least they had the experience of loving a creature to death and having it treat them like an idiot.

Cokie Roberts is a senior news analyst for National Public Radio, and a special correspondent for ABC News. Her reports and news analyses can be heard regularly on NPR's newsmagazine show "Morning Edition." She won the esteemed Edward R. Murrow Award from the Corporation for Public Broadcasting in 1990, and she has written for *The New York Times Magazine* and the *Atlantic Monthly*.

Richard Scarry

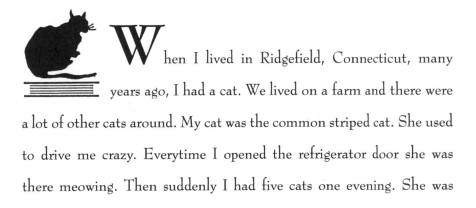

When I lived in Ridgefield, Connecticut, many years ago, I had a cat. We lived on a farm and there were a lot of other cats around. My cat was the common striped cat. She used to drive me crazy. Everytime I opened the refrigerator door she was there meowing. Then suddenly I had five cats one evening. She was sitting on my lap when she went into labor. I managed to get her into the barn in time.

I have neighbors' cats in Switzerland; they are very good at keeping my lawn free of moles.

My favorite cats are lions. I go to Kenya frequently and have seen hundreds of them. We once drove in our Volkswagen bus with a sun roof. A lioness was sleeping in a tree (some lions can climb trees, but not all). The lioness fell out of the tree through the sunroof into the bus. She was more frightened than we were. The driver opened the door and let the lioness out, and was given a medal for his quick thinking and bravery.

Lions copulate as much as 360 times in one week—every twenty to thirty minutes. At the end of each session the lion will roar and bite the back of the lioness's head. That's why so many lionesses have chewed-up ears.

A note about lion cubs: the male will eat them if hungry and there is nothing else around. So much for lions.

I like cheetahs, too. In Tanzania, I once took a long walk with a young cheetah. She was an orphaned pet at the lodge where I was staying. It was like taking a walk with a frisky pet dog. They too can climb trees a bit, but only when they are young. I also like wart-hogs, but they belong in another book.

Cats like me. I visited a friend the other day. She has a cat. She had never seen me before. I sat on the couch. That cat came right over and sat on my lap. I am irresistible.

My favorite literary cat is Huckle Cat. He wears lederhosen. He has a sister named Sally and he has a father and mother. His best friend is Lowly Worm. He has appeared in more copies of books than any other cat in history—and that includes the Owl and the Pussycat.

Yesterday a neighbor's all-black cat crossed in front of me. Yesterday was a very lucky day.

Richard Scarry is an award-winning children's writer and illustrator. He lives in Gstaad, Switzerland.

Susan Fromberg Schaeffer

I acquired my first cat because a friend told me that if I got one I would stop getting involved with unsuitable men. So, she gave me this wild cat that grew up in the woods of Massachusetts. He turned out to be an extremely jealous cat and attacked men who came into the house. When I met the man I finally married, the cat only took little swipes at him, so I took this to be a good sign.

My current cat is probably the second great cat love of my life. He's seven years old and his name is Foudini. He's named after the magician in the "Lucky Pup Show," a TV program that was on in 1949. At first, the cat had no idea what petting was for. If I tried to pet him he looked at me suspiciously. It took him two years to realize he could sit on a person's lap. He made very gradual progress. He would come close to me, lean part of his head on my thigh, and look at me to see if it was all right. Then a little more of him would come on to me, and finally he actually got onto my lap.

Foudini is a one-person cat and sleeps with me. When my husband gets into bed, the cat won't move, so my husband put his hand under him and moves him over the way you'd move an egg in a frying pan with a spatula. Then he gets into bed also, but the cat is clearly convinced that the bed is his place, and it's an outrage that someone else gets to share the bed.

Foudini types rows of Js on the computer. He spends a lot of time sitting on the armrest of my chair trying to figure out what's so interesting about what I'm doing. After many minutes, he sticks out a paw and puts it on the keyboard. He always hits the J key. He'll fill the screen with Js, and he loves to watch them jump across the screen. He usually manages to fill up three screens with Js before I remove him from the computer. The Js must look like insects to him, and he seems very pleased with himself. When I shout at him, he'll stop, but then he'll come back and do it again. Then he has to be put out of the room.

It does seem that there is some type of ESP between cats and people. If you want a cat to jump, you look at the cat and then at the place you want it to jump to; it will understand and do it.

The first cat I ever came across belonged to an ex-fiancé. At that point, I thought I didn't like cats, since we'd had a dog growing up, and I had heard this particular cat praised incessantly for its detachment and its independence. It seemed to me that you would be just as happy with a rock as this cat. I spent one summer at this man's lake house, and became quite fed up with the entire family. There was a large crawl space above a closet, and I discovered it was the one place I could find some privacy and no one would know where I was. So I crawled into the crawl space and there was the cat, so well-known for his indifference to human beings. I started petting him, and he was absolutely beside himself with joy. At the time, I had very long hair and I used hair spray on it. After a good deal of my petting, the cat started to try to wash my hair as if it were fur. He couldn't quite understand why, as he washed it, it never seemed to come to an end. Obviously he didn't like the taste of the spray because he shook his head and made dreadful faces, but he was determined to finish.

After that the cat and I were the best of friends. This provoked considerable disgust in the rest of the family, who wanted to think that this cat could manage quite well without any human affection, when he was obviously starved for it. I think that my fascination with cats began in that crawl space.

This Christmas, somebody sent me a book called *Cat Dependent No More*. I wrote back and said I would love to read it, but my cat wouldn't let me. Cats haven't run my house, but Foudini comes pretty close to running me. He always wants to sleep in our bed, but at three or four in the morning, he also wants to get up and go out. When he was younger, if I didn't get up, he would start knocking things off the dresser. He would go from small things, such as jewelry, which I would ignore, to larger things, which I would then hear moving toward the edge of the dresser—books or bottles of perfume. Then I had to get up and let him out. Now he screams when he wants to leave, and he sets up such a racket that you have to put him out or he'll wake everyone up.

Writers have to spend a lot of time by themselves in small, closed spaces. Cats are happy in small, closed spaces, and they provide patient company for writers that most other beings can't provide.

Susan Fromberg Schaeffer is a novelist and poet living in Brooklyn, where she is a professor at Brooklyn College. Her novels include the bestselling *The Madness of a Seduced Woman, Buffalo Afternoon,* and *Green Island.*

Charles Simic

I have two cats, both females. If you live in the country, as we do, you need cats to do what cats do best: catch mice. "They're vicious killers," my son says, "who disguise themselves as two friendly, slightly overweight kitties."

Cookie is eleven. She came from God knows where. We believe

summer people abandoned her. We took her in when she was a kitten. I think she was separated from her mother before she learned proper kitty manners. She doesn't know that she is supposed to retract her claws when playing. Try that on a mother cat, and she'll let you have it. Cookie is an affectionate cat, but watch out! She'll scratch you badly. Otherwise, she is a great talker. If you ask her, "Cookie, how are you doing today?" she'll meow right back. Whenever you speak to her she replies. She could go on the "MacNeil-Lehrer Newshour." She's made more sense than some of the guests they have there.

The other cat is a young cat we got from some people down the road. Her name is Josephine. She's all black and has huge eyes. She seems to be in a state of permanent astonishment. She hardly ever meows, but her eyes say: This is an incredible world! She's a great mouser. We spent our mornings in the summer removing corpses from our front door. When there are no more mice to kill, she goes after moles, snakes, and birds.

The cats like to sit on my page when I read or write. Cookie has a loud purrer, as if she needs a new muffler. I shove her away and she comes right back. You know how it is: you pet the cat and you forget what you were going to say.

I've had many cats and they have all been different. Cats invite us to pay attention. They're fascinating to watch. They're beautiful, mysterious, inscrutable, and yet after a while one begins to know their individual temperaments by the slightest nuances in their behavior and the expression in their eyes. We have a dog, a gregarious local mutt, and he is much easier to read, of course. Cats teach us that it takes a lot of looking before we begin to see things in front of our eyes. As a writer I'm always so much in my head that it's a relief to look at a cat.

The cats don't run the household as much as Smokie, the dog, does. In the summer they mostly ignore us and stay outdoors. But, a strange thing has come over us since our kids have grown up and left home. It's idiotic, but we may, on a trip walking down Fifth Avenue, find ourselves saying to each other, "I wonder what Cookie and Josephine are doing?"

The cat is the unknown in the house. If life is an algebraic equation, then the cat is the X. Here's a creature that's been around for thousands of years and hasn't changed much. If you watch lions, tigers, and leopards, you see that they pretty much do the same thing the house cat does. For example, the way they lick themselves and fight.

Obviously, the original model was so terrific that they have no intention of changing anything. They're the original conservatives. To hell with Darwin! The foolish monkeys came down from the trees and became human beings; the cats, smart as they are, stayed in the tree yawning at the entire spectacle.

Why is one attracted to cats? I really don't know. I like dogs, too. One admires a cat's independence, its selfishness, its narcissism. It's really difficult to say one is loved in turn by a cat. The relationship is much more complex. One often knows one's cat better than one knows one's relatives. Do we communicate, the cats and I? Of course we do. Here is a language without words. Truly, to communicate all you need are four eyes.

I don't remember anything about the plot, but there's a wonderful scene with an eighteenth-century writer in an old Peter Sellers movie. The writer, wearing a powdered wig, is seen passionately writing with a quill. A little black kitten is sitting on the desk. He finishes writing, and while reading over what he has written, absentmindedly picks up the kitten, blots the wet ink, and puts it back exactly where it was. There's your writer and the cat.

Here's a poem by a contemporary Yugoslav poet, Novica Tadic, which I just translated:

Cat Strike

At night the cat's cough wakes him up.
He sits up, gets out of bed.
Puts on his robe since it's cold.
Puts on his slippers since his feet are bare.
Slowly steps to the window.
Pushes aside the curtain, looks out, sees:
Down below.
The length of the avenue,
All the way to the Square of the Republic,
Thousands and thousands of phosphorescent flames,
Thousands and thousands of cats,
Thousands and thousands of raised tails.

Calmly
He draws the curtains together.
Returns to his warm bed.
Yawns once,
Says:
The cats are on strike.

Charles Simic is a poet living in Strafford, New Hampshire. His awards include a Guggenheim Fellowship, two fellowships from the National Endowment for the Arts, a National Book Award nomination, a MacArthur Fellowship, and the Pulitzer Prize for Poetry in 1990.

Sharon Sheehe Stark

To me, cats are almost like angels. I had my favorite cat, Beau, only three months. He was a tuxedo cat—all black with a white bib and paws—and appeared in the dead of winter three years ago. I was on crutches after I fell on the ice and shattered my hip. He was very sick and I debated whether I should let him in because we already had four cats and three dogs. My husband said, "No way," and then he foolishly went off to work. An hour later, I took the cat to the vet, and in a week or so he was in good health. He was the most loving, wonderful cat, and he never left my side. I was totally smitten. When spring came he started inching back outside, going out for short spells, and then one day he left and didn't come back. I took it very hard.

One day, I got a phone call from a neighbor who told me she heard I had a new cat. She said it sounded like Mr. Sneakers, who had lived with her six years and then one day just up and walked out on her. She described him, and I said, that's Beau, and I told her my story. She sighed. "Oh dear," she said. "Mr. Sneakers broke your heart, too." It turned out he was a riverboat gambler of a cat who had about seven of us spinning in circles. We were all madly in love with him. He would hang around just long enough to steal our hearts, and then he jilted us, every one. But this cat had such a dynamic personality that we were all hooked on him for life. Just about a month ago, he was killed, and we all went into mourning. His first love, Susan, was devastated for weeks, even though Sneakers had left her many years before.

I have three cats now: J.C., Susie Q, and White Job. This last cat appeared out of nowhere, and my husband said, "What are we going to do with that white job?" So White Job she is.

I only became an animal person twelve years ago, with a beagle stray that I still have, and after that, the world just assorted to versions of a beagle named Chinka. I'd see birds as flying Chinkas and cows as big Chinkas and bugs as winged Chinkas, and so on. Then the cats started coming. I converted from a dog person to a cat person, although I can't quite put my finger on when, or how, that conversion took place.

I put a cat in nearly every story, and the minute I sit down to write they're involved in the process. I had one cat who typed; she was trying to help me write my first cat story. And, of course, when I'm revising, they sit on the printed page, while I scribble under bellies, between paws.

In my stories, I pattern a lot of little old lady characters after my cats: a certain sharp-eyed, no-nonsense, secretive character that keeps popping up again and again. My mother-in-law was very catlike, and after awhile she actually began to look like a cat. With writing, you combine many elements—some merely catalytic—and if you are steeped in cat magic, it'll show up in your writing sooner or later.

My cats like to sleep on my back, and one time I woke up in the middle of the night, terrified. I thought I had developed a heart murmur. But of course it was only White Job, purring away.

I live in the country, so I never actually went looking for a cat. When we lose a cat, within twenty-four hours, quite miraculously, another one turns up at the front door.

Of course they run my house. All day I open and shut doors. I have my household organized in ways that most people would not approve of. I have two cats that eat on the table so that the dog can't steal their dinner. This means that most of the time I can't eat at the table. Usually, I dine standing up. My beagle, who's quite clever, has figured out that if she tugs on the tablecloth, the cats' dishes eventually tumble to the floor.

J.C. is a loner cat who must eat by herself or not at all. I had another cat who had to eat in the back room with the door shut tight. If I forgot to close it, she'd nag me until I complied. I recently lost a lot of weight, and I think one of the reasons is because I was misjudging the amount that I was actually taking in. I'd make myself a sandwich, and you know how it goes: a bite for me, then a bite for you; a bite for you, a bite for you; a spoon of ice cream for me, then a spoon for you, a spoon for you, and a spoon for you.

I'd like to be able to think like a cat; I'd like to be that subtle and mysterious. Everything I am is on my face, so maybe that's what appeals to me about them, they're so unlike me. Cats are what I aspire to. I'd like to be able to hide from the world and keep my secrets to myself.

My mother recently went to a friend's funeral. In the old woman's casket was her pet cat. It had been stuffed and fixed in a sitting position, staring adoringly at the deceased. I assume the stuffing was done some months in advance, with this particular event in mind. I trust, too, the cat died a natural death.

Sharon Sheehe Stark is the author of the novel *A Wrestling Season* and the short-story collection *The Dealers' Yard and Other Stories*. She lives in rural Pennsylvania.

Donald E. Westlake

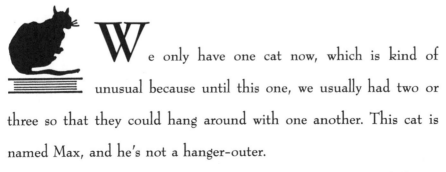

We only have one cat now, which is kind of unusual because until this one, we usually had two or three so that they could hang around with one another. This cat is named Max, and he's not a hanger-outer.

From the time he was a kitten, Max was independent in a different way—a tough-guy cat. He will be in the same room with you, but he will not look at you—none of that love stuff. It took us about a week to figure out his name, but we thought, if this were a person he would smoke a cigar, and so we named him Max.

We don't let Max run the house, although he would like to be in charge of food distribution. He's never given up that dream, but we simply ignore him. Except under extreme duress, he doesn't speak. If he feels we should be feeding him, he will sit in the corner and look at me, and occasionally he'll walk over to me and around me, then he'll go back to the corner and look at me, but he won't speak and he won't complain. He's saying, You know what your responsibilities are. He keeps it at a dignified level.

Once we had three cats, two males and a female. The female was named Emily and was one of the most evil creatures on the face of the earth. Fortunately, she kept to herself most of the time. Cats, as you know, when they catch a mouse, like to play with it. They like to go away and then come back and play with it again. But it's usually dead or gone when they come back. Emily would catch a mouse and put it in the bathtub in the kids' bathroom specifically so that she could play with it. Then she would go away, and when she came back it would still be there. She turned the bathtub into a stalag and the kids hated it; they'd get up in the morning and find mouse parts in the tub.

Emily's personality has shown up in some of the evil characters I've written, but the kids all had a soft spot for her. Once she got sick and went to the vet, who said they would know if she would die or get better in three days. So, I suggested, if it turned out she would die, we'd take her to a taxidermist, have her stuffed, and put her behind the refrigerator, where she lives anyway, so that we could go over there and say, "Hi Emily," and she'd ignore me the way she does anyway. Nobody liked that suggestion. Emily ended up living. I put up with her for fifteen years, which is the only indication that I'm a saint.

The two male cats, named Johnny and Maurice, were like Laurel and Hardy, or Ralph and Norton. Johnny was the smart one—a strong, powerful cat—and Maurice was the nerd. He was such a dimwit. Johnny was the boss cat, but he was never mean. He knew he had a retarded brother. There was a sweetness to their relationship.

Maurice had a great fascination with water. If the kitchen sink had a slow drip, he would study it for hours. He would get into the sink and watch the drip form and then hit. He would slowly get drenched, but he was so absorbed in learning the secrets of water he didn't care. Like that great Gene Wilder line, "I'm hysterical and I'm wet," Maurice would suddenly realize he was wet and run away.

When I was a kid, my parents never let me have a pet, until I was eleven, when my mother won an argument with my father that I didn't know about. She said, "The next time he wants something for a pet, let him have it." I didn't know that this was waiting for me. I had a paper route, and one family on my route had a cat that just had kittens. Shortly after they were born, a tomcat came along and started making real trouble with the kittens, but there was this one kitten who ran underneath the tomcat and began chewing on his hind legs, as if to say, "Leave my brother alone!" The tomcat kept looking around and couldn't figure out where this was coming from. It scared him and he ran away. The family there had been asking everyone if they wanted a kitten. I asked, can I have the one who scared off the tomcat because I figured I could use that as an argument with my parents, like, "Here is this hero cat—someday he'll save us when the house is on fire." So, I took him home and, as I started to plead, my parents said, "It's okay, you can have it." Then my mother told me about their agreement, and I must admit that at that moment I was so sad I hadn't brought a dog, because whatever I brought is what I would get.

Recently, my wife was at the vet, who treats only cats. She was sitting in the lobby when a woman came in, walked over to the receptionist, and announced that she was there for Attila's Valium. The whole waiting room cracked up, and when I heard that I thought, if you wanted him calm you should have named him something else.

I don't think cats are psychic. When they sit and stare at a doorway and there's nothing in it, there's nothing in it.

The main thing that's wrong with cats is that they don't take no for an answer. I'm like that sometimes, but they're more persistent than I am.

Donald E. Westlake is the author of thirty-five novels, as well as twenty others under the name of Richard Stark, and five more under the name of Tucker Coe. His screenplay adaptation of the Jim Thompson novel *The Grifters* was nominated for an Oscar. He lives in Manhattan and upstate New York.

Kate Wilhelm

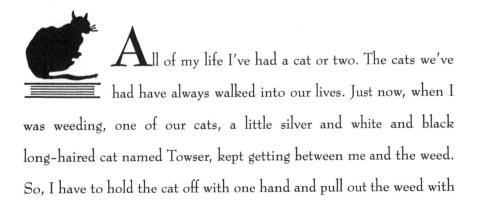All of my life I've had a cat or two. The cats we've had have always walked into our lives. Just now, when I was weeding, one of our cats, a little silver and white and black long-haired cat named Towser, kept getting between me and the weed. So, I have to hold the cat off with one hand and pull out the weed with

the other. No matter how I push the cat away, the cat keeps coming back, purr, purr, purr. They're difficult to discourage.

We've never gone out looking for a cat; they've always come to us. Our first cat appeared on our doorstep one winter, with snow up to the eaves and bitter cold outside. We heard scratching at the door and this pitiful crying, and we opened the door and there was a cat. We named her Cleo because she used to stretch out on the couch with one paw behind her head and blink her eyes lazily. She *was* Cleopatra.

Right now we have four cats. Towser thinks there can be no reason why I would be outside except to pet her. So, she follows me around and always manages to be between me and what I'm trying to do. We have one cat who's a tortoiseshell, named Pumpkin. She is probably our most beautiful cat. She hates to be petted and held, yet she craves it at the same time. She'll come over and say, "Pet me, pet me, but don't touch me." This makes it a little awkward. We pet her, but we're very careful not to touch her stomach or various areas where she says, "If you do, I'll bite you."

We also have a male tiger cat named Chip. When Chip was a kitten, my son let him sleep draped across his shoulders. And now he's a thirty-pound cat who has never realized it's one thing to be a kitten on the shoulders and another thing to be a thirty-pound cat. And he terrifies guests because he's very fond of strangers and wants to get on their shoulders. Our fourth cat is a black, long-haired cat whose name is either Beast or Monster. He answers to both.

I write a mystery series with two detectives, a man and wife team who are both retired. She was a psychologist and he was a New York City detective, and they now live in upstate New York and get called on all kinds of cases. They also have three cats who are remarkably like our cats. So, yes, I watch their behavior quite closely; it all is used one way or another. Other characters I've written about have had cats, but it's never been this ongoing thing like it is in the mystery series.

I don't let my cats in the office anymore because I've gone to a computer. I have found that a kitten or cat on a typewriter keyboard is one thing, but the same beast on a computer keyboard is quite something else. I haven't lost anything, but I've had a lot of garbage. If I see a lot of garbage on the screen, I realize, oh yes, a cat has walked on the keyboard, leaving a cat trail behind.

Two of our cats really like brewer's yeast. Years ago, I read somewhere that brewer's yeast will help control fleas. So, we went to brewer's yeast and two of the cats became real addicts. They need their fix at least twice a day, and they get their way because a cat who wants something is not tolerable. They get what they want pretty much. But they don't sleep with me; I can't bear a cat purring in my ear or walking across my stomach when I'm trying to sleep, and they like to do both.

Mehitabel is my favorite literary cat; I love when she says life is just one damn kitten after another.

I don't know of anybody who knows how a cat thinks. I think they're absolutely inscrutable and wonderful because of that. A cat gazing at you: is it thinking of yeast, is it thinking of the last mouse it caught? There's a wonderful B. Kliban cartoon of a cat staring in the corner, and the owner going through what I just did, "What is that cat thinking?" And the little balloon over the cat's head shows what it's thinking: the corner.

I'm looking at a cat sleeping right now with its paw draped across his eyes because of the way the light is coming through the door. I like their independence. I don't like obsequious people or animals, and if the cat wants something, it's a demand. It's not all this tail-wagging and drooling; it's give it to me now or I'll bite you.

We lived in a big old Victorian house in Milford, Pennsylvania. Of course, the house was haunted. We also had a dog at the time. The dog never had a clue about the house, but the cats all knew. We would have guests who would hear things in the night, and they would say they would see the cat looking at nothing, just staring, and the dog would be asleep two feet away, totally unaware. He hadn't heard the noises; didn't know what was there; didn't know he should be looking at something. The difference was so apparent. The cats knew, but they didn't much care that the house was haunted; they just thought it was interesting.

Not all cats are psychic; some are as bright as dishwater. We had cats who knew exactly when it was time for children to come home from school and they'd be near the door waiting, or knew exactly when it was time for someone to come home in the car and they'd get up on the windowsill. And this is a family of nonhabits. If my husband goes out, I never know when he's going to come back, but I've had cats who knew.

Kate Wilhelm is a science fiction writer living in Eugene, Oregon.

Nancy Willard

We've always had cats. We have two now. One is called Kasper; he's gray and has one eye because he was hit by a car. I don't see that as a handicap, because Odin, the Norse god of wisdom, was supposed to have traded one eye for wisdom. I like to think that Kasper has some special powers because he only has one eye.

The other cat is named Thumbs. He has six toes, and he's very fat.

Do you know why some cats lose an eye when they're hit by a car? Someone told me that when a dog is hit by a car, it's likely to have a leg broken because it turns and runs when it sees a car coming. A cat will stand out of bravery to face the car, which it views as the enemy. This is why so many cats lose an eye when they're hit by a car. But our cat doesn't know he's handicapped in any way; he doesn't hunt mice, he hunts grasshoppers and moths.

I once had a Maine coon cat named Owl. He liked to sit in front of the house, and he was so large that once somebody asked me, "Is that a cat or a dog?" He had a very broad, owl-like face, and used to get into terrible fights. When cats fight they go for the eyes. In one fight, he had one eyelid badly torn, so we took him to the vet. The veterinarian stitched the eyelid, but he told us that in order to make this cat with its one eye not seem vulnerable to other cats, he was going to make a little stitch on the eyelid and sew a button on it. Owl looked like a Raggedy Ann doll. The sight of him could stop people in their tracks—a cat going down the street with one good eye and a button.

I grew up with two cats and a dog. I think cats take care of us as much as we take care of them. Our nickname for Kasper is Nurse Kasper, because if anyone in the house is ill, the cat stays in the room at the foot of the bed until the person is well. I just finished writing a book about a cat that has the power to heal, called *The Tortilla Cat*, based on Kasper. I'm sure we all think we get better quicker because of this cat.

I think that after cats are with us for a long period of time they know much more about us than we know about them. I would love to see the world through a cat's eyes. In almost all of my books, cats are the guardians of those who take care of them. Exactly how cats understand what we need and what we want is a mystery.

Somebody once told me that six-toed cats are psychic. I make a lot of soft sculptures. Once, I was working on the figure of an angel, and I needed some feathers for the wings. So, I said within hearing of our cat, Thumbs, "Gee, I wish I had some feathers about five inches long." The next morning there were two piles of feathers in the kitchen—an assortment, just what I needed. I put two and two together. Two days later, I said, "What I really need are some red feathers." The cat went out and killed a cardinal.

Then, my son—who was in third grade at the time—wanted to try it. He said, "Okay, Thumbs, bring me a mole for breakfast." It took the cat a couple of days to catch one, but when the cat brought the mole, he put it right by my son's chair at breakfast. Then my husband tried. He said, "Thumbs, get me a squirrel." And because he had asked in a skeptical tone, the cat brought in a live squirrel and let it go in the house.

For a long time, we didn't ask for anything because we began to think it was spooky. But when my son came home a couple of years ago from college, he said, "I wonder if Thumbs still has this power. Thumbs, bring me something." I said, "Don't bring . . ." and I went on to name everything that cat had ever brought into the house. I said, "Bring us no birds, no bats, no squirrels, no moles." I covered the field. The next day, the cat brought in a frog. Where did he find a frog? We don't even live near water. It was the only thing I hadn't named. Now we watch what we say. You have to be careful of what you say around cats. They're aware of us in ways we're hardly aware of.

Cats are very independent. They can be very present while I work, but they won't disturb me. They will disturb me if they're hungry or want to go out. A cat can walk over a desk crowded with a manuscript and pens and disturb absolutely nothing, unless it wants something, in which case it knocks everything to the floor. They have respect for order, or one's version of order.

It's not true that all cats don't like water. We used to have a cat that got into the bathtub with people. We had to warn guests. It can be quite a shock to be taking a bath and have a cat join you.

I love to find out how people choose the names for their cats. It often has to do with how they found the cat, or the look of the cat. Maybe the cat has a way of letting you know what its real name is.

Nancy Willard is the author of thirty books of poetry and fiction for adults and children. *A Visit to William Blake's Inn* won the 1982 Newbery Medal for that year's most distinguished contribution to children's literature. In 1989, her book of poems *Walter Walker* was nominated for the National Book Critics Circle Award. Her work has appeared in *The New Yorker* and *Esquire*. Her recent books include *A Nancy Willard Reader* and *Pish, Posh, Said Hieronymus Bosch*. She is a Lecturer in English at Vassar College.

180

The Cat

on My

Shoulder